DETOX YOUR EGO

STEVEN SYLVESTER

<u>**headline**</u>

First published in Great Britain in 2016
by HEADLINE PUBLISHING GROUP

1

Cataloguing in Publication Data is available from the British Library

Trade Paperback ISBN 978 1 4722 2733 1
Paperback ISBN 978 1 4722 2735 5

Typeset in Serifa BT Light

Printed and bound in Great Britain by
Clays Ltd, St Ives plc

Headline's policy is to use papers that are natural, renewable and
recyclable products and made from wood grown in well-managed forests
and other controlled sources. The logging and manufacturing processes are
expected to conform to the environmental regulations of the country of origin.

HEADLINE PUBLISHING GROUP
An Hachette UK Company
Carmelite House
50 Victoria Embankment
London EC4Y 0DZ
www.headline.co.uk
www.hachette.co.uk

Contents

$\bullet\ \bullet\ \bullet$

Part Four: How to Detox Your Ego

Part Five: Inner Ego Programme

(What You Tell Yourself – Hidden to Others)

Part Six: Outer Ego Programme

(What You Tell Yourself – Seen by Others)

Part Seven: Transformational Ego Programme

(How You Can Serve Others)

Acknowledgements

• • •

I want to take this time to express my sincere appreciation to Jonathan Taylor and his team at Headline Publishing for believing in this book.

I'd also like to thank all the people that I've ever spent time with for sharing their innermost thoughts and experiences that have helped shape my approach.

I am blessed to share special time with my wonderful family & friends, especially my Mum & Dad – Jenny & Scott and my in-laws Eve & Peter – thank you for your love, wisdom and guidance.

And to my wife Claudia, you are truly my soul mate – thank you for always giving me your love and time unconditionally. To our beautiful children Zak, Isabella, Blake and Noah – thank you for your valuable input and allowing me the time away to write this book. You are my inspiration and I love each of you with all my heart.

Summary

• • •

Part one outlines why you should **Detox Your Ego**. It charts the importance of understanding what you tell yourself, especially under pressure. Key learning is highlighted. Take time for reflection with the *stop, look and listen* sections throughout the book.

Part two overviews my discovery of the **Detox Your Ego** process. I summarise my early career as a professional cricketer in terms of my initial feelings, thoughts and experiences.

Part three highlights the important findings about ego when working with world champions.

Part four explains the process ahead, showing the Leadership withoutEGO® model I developed that arose from working with both world champions and other elite athletes.

Parts five, **six and seven** present the **Detox Your Ego** programme. Each stage takes you on a journey of self-discovery regarding how your ego impacts your life. You will assess the way you win and lose in life, by examining your level of selfishness and selflessness. You will also unravel your emotional pain when you are doing something important.

In **part seven** you will be tasked to build your own personal legacy by increasing your clarity, contribution and purpose. As a result such self-awareness will enable you to self-correct your level of selfishness in life. You will see how your identity has formed and how your self-regard has developed. You will understand much better how conflicts and contradictions manifest in your life. The aim will be for you to increase your ability to operate without ego or self-lessly in order to be happier, freer and more successful in life.

PART ONE

Why Detox Your Ego?

1

My Challenge to You

• • •

I want you to question your approach to life. Our normal assumptions about winning and losing need to be challenged. We take winning for granted, striving to win in what we do regardless of what it is. Why? Why is winning important to us? What need does winning address – what urge does it satisfy?

Detox Your Ego provides a very different perspective regarding winning. This book is an easy-to-follow seven-step guide to reveal how *your* ego impacts on *your* life, and provides a catalyst for a deeper reflection on doing things differently.

In this programme, our automatic goal of winning is turned on its head. Instead, you will discover how your ego drives interference in what you do. *Detox Your Ego* suggests individuals should nurture a new way of thinking in order to be happy and gain success in life. Are you up for the challenge?

By conducting a detox of your ego, especially under intense pressure, you will be able to execute a skill or task with greater ease, mastery and success. I will show you how this has been achieved across a number of successful people in sport, business and life.

However, this is not a sports book. Here, sport is used as a metaphor for life so, although there are sporting examples across the book, they are used to facilitate learning for you – regardless of what you do. Business executives are also highlighted for the same reason: to facilitate learning. This book gives examples of how athletes, business executives and everyone can operate using a different lens to look through for ultimate freedom, happiness and success in life.

2

An Invitation

• • •

This book is an invitation for you to be completely open to *what you tell yourself*. Do any of the following sound familiar to you? *'I'm struggling with this . . .'*, or, *'I'm so angry with my inconsistent results . . .'*, or, *'Winning is not enough . . .'* Regardless of what you do, I want to invite you to see the dangers of becoming too self-centred in life.

Detox Your Ego contains provocative and challenging new ways of thinking about *what you tell yourself* – your ego – about the approach you take to winning and losing in life. It is for those with a desire to help themselves feel freer, happier and more successful in what they do. This is not an easy journey of self-discovery, and you will be faced with uncomfortable truths about how *you* get in the way of what *you* do. It requires you to be open and flexible about confronting your deeply held beliefs about winning. In this way you will be able to reveal what choices you make and what your personal truth is.

I have found through both personal experience and working with others that wanting to win is driven by our need to boost our self-esteem and confidence. We wittingly or unwittingly become selfish as we see winning for oneself as the purpose for living. Unfortunately, such a selfish attitude leads to a life of conflict. In contrast, I have discovered that when someone focuses on winning for a team or community they become freer, happier, and have a clarity of purpose that leads to ultimate success.

I would like to invite you to increase your understanding of your own ego, so that you may be able to transform yourself and the lives of those around you. If you are willing and committed to entering a personal journey of deep transformation in the way you think, feel and act, then I would encourage you to read on and enjoy the journey.

3

The Art of Becoming Open

• • •

When you read this book's title, 'Detox Your Ego', what did you feel? What reaction did it cause? Did you feel immediate interest or discomfort with any aspect of it? Did you either get completely absorbed by the notion of detoxing your ego? Or did you immediately dismiss it as a load of rubbish? Alternatively, did you experience any contradictory feeling – that is, wanting to reject it while also holding some curiosity about it?

Regardless of whether you are open or closed, or experience some contrary views, it doesn't matter; this book is for you. It will help you gain a deeper appreciation of your ego and its impact on your life. Being open to the title is a perfect starting point, as it means you want to know more, as you appreciate that we all have egos. In contrast, being closed to the title is also a great way to kick things off. This book is about learning to understand what you take for granted; I believe being open enhances our happiness and that we shouldn't deny ourselves this gift.

Detoxing your ego is about you looking at yourself in a different way; detox means to 'get rid of something', while ego means 'a sense of self-importance'. This book aims to help you 'get rid of self interest – especially when you are

, therefore, take you on a
ive impact of winning and
way of doing things.

out right or wrong, nor about
out entering a process of planned
of interconnected steps, to deeply
xperience with all its subjectivity and
ate a much wider debate about how we
pursu   d how we can better contribute more to
society. Th   this process, I urge you to develop an open
and reflective style over your own narrative in order to create
change. It is about building your self-awareness using the
Leadership withoutEGO® model within this book. Remember:
becoming open is not an easy process. However it is essential
if you are going to significantly improve your life.

4

Learn to Stop, Look and Listen

· · ·

I'm sure you can remember the old TV road safety advert –
stop, look and listen – when children were encouraged to
stop, look and listen to see if there was any traffic coming
in order to know when it was safe to walk across the road.
Children were asked to slow down, not to rush or run across
the road; instead they were encouraged to take time to assess
the danger of moving traffic and reduce the high accident
rate.

So that you can detox your ego, this book aims to help you
stop, look and listen to your inner voice. You will be invited to
ask yourself the following two critical questions:

STOP **1. STOP: LOOK: LISTEN**

What do *you tell yourself* in a pressurised situation?

Is your reaction or response driven by selfishness or
selflessness?

These are difficult questions to answer. You will need to take time to explore them and understand where you are at any one time. During each of the Seven Steps you will be invited to reflect on the key question being asked; each one of these will enable you to do this as you reflect on what you are being asked.

As you read on, you will find there are forty Stop, Look and Listen points for reflection. I have found that the most effective way to use these points is to initially take time for self-reflection by either noting things down or by underlining the points that you want to refer back to. This is helpful as it's not about your views being right or wrong; it is about simply knowing where you are, what is going on in your life that you are happy with, and what you are not happy with.

I have found that, when we gain a greater insight into whom we are and what we do, we become freer, and that such greater freedom automatically increases our happiness. By increasing our happiness we choose to become more successful with whatever we are doing.

Unfortunately, we have learnt to ignore what we tell ourselves (our ego) and we ignore our emotional world at our peril. By accessing our emotional world, we are in a much better position to unlock our fears. Unlocking our fears is the key to our freedom and happiness, especially when we are doing something critical. When you start to examine your ego (what you tell yourself about yourself) you will be able to look below the surface to reveal your emotions and fears. You will be able to see what is truly holding you back in life. Such self-awareness is key to seeing how fear is manifested in our emotions, attitude, behaviour, values and beliefs.

I now know my ego was one of the major reasons for my

own career in professional cricket stalling, and I wanted to know why. Working with world champions enabled me to learn something about myself and my ego, or selfishness. I will draw on my extensive first-hand experiences as a professional sportsman and now a chartered psychologist to show how I have helped athletes, some of whom have become world champions using this philosophy.

Importantly, this is not a book written by someone without an ego. Like all of us, I do have an ego; for many years I didn't realise how it impacted me and held me back from performing at my best. After twenty years of experience of consulting with world champions and taking time to study the ego, I can see its damaging effects. Today, I'm acutely aware how it can negatively impact my decision-making, and how to help others benefit from my experiences. I've been through my own ego detox, and continue to revisit each step of the programme as a matter of course throughout my life, especially when difficulties arise.

All references to people I've worked with throughout this book will remain confidential and anonymous. In addition, all those involved in the storytelling have given their consent for the story to be told. My aim is to hold your focus on the model and the seven questions across Seven Steps, in order to specifically help you and avoid you becoming side-tracked by the personalities involved.

We don't usually spend time thinking about what we tell ourselves, so if the questions you are faced with stir feelings and emotions that you find difficult to deal with, then please find someone to confide in or consult with your GP.

2. STOP: LOOK: LISTEN

How regularly do you take time for self-reflection?

Remember to take time for reflection in order to gain the maximum benefit from each Step.

The Discovery of Detox Your Ego

5

Winning for One's Self

• • •

I grew up in total admiration of one particular cricket player's charisma and performance. I played many a Test match in our back garden with my older brother, who I was determined to beat, across the long hot summers of my childhood, when I would try to mimic my hero. Typically my brother and I would only break to have a quick drink and clock the latest scores in the Test match or World Cup playing at that particular time.

We would then return to our large back garden to resume play. We had created our own cricket surface – or strip – as well as using the rest of the garden for our run ups. I loved beating my brother at cricket. My father would often come to the back door, which had a staircase down to the garden. He would stand at the railings and watch. I wanted to show him my skills and get his approval even as a small child. I tried to play like my hero as much as possible – I even mimicked his walk to the crease and his air of self-confidence.

As we progressed we started using proper cricket balls, which created a problem, damaging the garden fence as I smashed cover drives into it. My father was not best pleased as he took immense pride in his garden, even growing his own vegetable patch. We would make up rules about where the boundary lines were and often try to pinch the odd single and run two. At times we would get locked into fierce arguments, as a different view of the evidence would appear. A great piece of fielding where I would run, pick up the ball, throw and hit the stumps (in our case, the garden's plum tree), all in one movement, would create heated exchanges as I would appeal for a run out whilst my brother would argue that he got in. We would also debate the score, the overs, or what innings it was. Regardless of what it was, we were both so fixed on winning that the discussion took some time to resolve itself. I loved seeing the evidence that I could beat my older brother at something, especially when my father was watching.

I became a professional cricket player, but during my career I was blind to how my ego was interfering with my performance. Instead, I ruminated over why I could perform one day but not the next, but avoided the truth about my situation. For example, my first team and second team debuts were only a few weeks apart but the performances were dramatically different. I couldn't understand what stopped me being totally free to execute my skills with consistency on each and every occasion regardless of what team I was in.

The captain, a former England captain, was on the sidelines watching the match, my second team debut. I was totally excited about representing my county and I took three early wickets and it was like, 'Wow, this guy can bowl quick.' Four weeks later I made my first class debut and I got hit for 98 runs and didn't get a wicket in the entire match. That contrast was very disappointing and got me thinking. Why was there such a dramatic change in performance? What changed? My technique hadn't, so something else must have.

What were the differences? In my second team debut I was excited that my dream was coming true. I was overwhelmed that I had the chance to show my skills at this level. I felt that my purpose was simply to show what I could do at this new level. It was my first opportunity to play county cricket and my father and brother were alongside supporting me. Whilst I didn't know many of my teammates, I soon realised I was to open the bowling opposite one of my cricketing heroes – I felt privileged and positive to be playing alongside someone with such mastery. I also knew the opposition as I had already trialled at their club. It was a rain-affected match and so I had to wait for what felt like an eternity to play – this only heightened my desire to make an impression. I felt free and consistent. I was full of optimism, excitement and fun. There was a consistency between what others saw in me and what I was feeling inside. Just to be playing was great. I had no idea if I was good enough to play at this level. I had no contract and wasn't a professional cricketer at this stage. To my surprise my performance flowed freely and I did well. In fact, I was offered a professional contract on the basis of this one performance.

In contrast, four weeks later I was making my debut in the first team in first class county cricket. I now had signed the contract and was a fully fledged professional cricketer. I now had high expectations to perform and win. Clearly, I was pleased about making my first team debut but I tried to avoid how nervous I really was. I'd also been playing county cricket for a few weeks and had got to know a few of the guys – although not many in the first team. I was also on my own. I had no family members at the game, as it was taking place many miles from home. I felt tense but extremely happy to be playing and enjoying the start of a professional cricket-er's career. My thoughts were like being on a roller coaster

– up and down. Excited but worried about what might happen. I had a job to do now and desperately wanted to prove myself and not make any long-lasting errors. To my surprise my performance didn't flow and I didn't do well. In fact, I was dropped for the next game following this match.

My ego rushed in and out of my mind, like a tornado causing havoc and destruction. Will I survive and win? Or will this gale-force failure simply take me down as I make the choice to operate on the dark side? My tension, anxiety and insecurity were heightening as I learnt to survive. I became hijacked by my ego: *'what if this were to happen? . . .' 'what if that were to happen? . . .'* I entered an inner world of conflict, debate and distress. I was under enormous stress over what I was doing. I spent too much energy worrying about how my cricket was going and what others thought about me. I was too self-absorbed and not free to express myself. At the time, I didn't appreciate that the pursuit of winning for oneself had such a dangerous downside. Instead, I just thought it was all about the survival of the fittest and I just needed to work harder, be stronger and more dedicated to getting it right. However, the harder I tried, the worse my performance. I phoned my father to get his advice: 'You're wanting it too much,' he said, to which I would react strongly and say 'Of course'. Back then, I really didn't understand what he meant.

At the time, I had no real self-awareness over why my emotions and performances were different even though they were only a matter of weeks apart. I was left confused and frustrated. I found it difficult to understand why I couldn't express myself freely on each and every occasion. I felt my dream of playing professional cricket was turning into an absolute nightmare. I wondered why my greatest dream was fast becoming my greatest fear. I was riddled with thoughts of self-doubt about being good enough and worry over what others were thinking. I was blind to understanding my emotions and what I was avoiding. What am I not open to? What am I in conflict with? What is that 'something missing'? What was my personal truth? I was asking myself these questions but not able to generate any real answers.

Today, I'm in a better position to understand the dangers of winning for one's self. I am able to understand that I chose a more selfless perspective on my second team debut. Clearly, I didn't appreciate it at the time, but I was simply riding a wave of joy as I was in a unique position of representing my family in county cricket.

We were a close family unit that grew up loving the game, so playing county cricket was a privilege to all of us, especially my father, a good club cricketer who never got access to a higher level of the game. I felt supported by them and it was great to share in it with my family. I experienced delight as I could see the joy it gave them to share in this special moment. The family felt like it was going from obscurity to the professional game in one fell swoop. I was living my boyhood dream and making my family proud. I had a feeling that I was achieving something awesome for my community – my family, and my new county team. It made me feel so happy just being there to play in the match. It was wonderful to make those who loved me happy; an immense feeling of joy.

I now know that it was this happiness and sense of purpose that had unwittingly given me a real sense of freedom to perform at my best. If you are happy and contented you will perform with a high degree of freedom. If, however, you are unhappy you perform with a low degree of freedom.

I can now see and want to share the fact that winning for oneself is the quickest way to lose in whatever it is you are doing. It is not sustainable.

Throughout my cricketing career, I was unable to perform consistently, so after four years, a year playing in Australia and across two county cricket clubs, I decided to retire from the game. During this time, I had made only half a dozen first class appearances, but I'd played with – and against – world-class cricketers (and World Cup winners) from the West Indies, Pakistan and India, and I'd played at the home of cricket – Lord's. I'd learned from the best in the world. I used my experiences to help others, as I was determined to learn from my errors in the game.

 3. STOP: LOOK: LISTEN

Do you want to win for yourself?

Is winning at all costs your number one priority in life?

6

Conclusion:
Winning – a Warning

• • •

The pursuit of winning for one's self, should, like smoking, come with a government health warning:

'PURSUING WINNING FOR ONE'S SELF CAN SERIOUSLY DAMAGE YOUR HEALTH'

STOP **4. STOP: LOOK: LISTEN**

What is your reaction to such a statement?

Are you shocked?

Do you agree or disagree?

Are you indifferent to it?

I've had all sorts of responses, from 'what a load of rubbish' and instant dismissal, to surprise and shock – 'but tell me more'

What camp are you in?

Over the years, I have reached the conclusion that there is a human cost to the pursuit of winning. We completely underestimate the dangers of our pursuit of winning on our mental health. We get completely self-absorbed and self-centred as competing and beating others becomes central to how we live our lives. We have learnt that winning is good and is the key to our happiness and success.

On the surface, winning is everything. Our confidence and self worth are all derived from winning.

- Winners are seen positively and praised, while losers are seen negatively, criticised and ignored.
- Winners are put on pedestals and losers are forgotten.
- Winners are seen as role models and people to follow while losers are seen as nobodies.
- Winners are blind to their errors while losers over-analyse theirs.
- Winners avoid losing, and those they think are losers, while losers feel like victims, alienated and lost.
- Winning enables us to value and hold what is dear to our hearts.
- Winning adds meaning to our lives.
- Winning makes us feel great and builds our identity and self esteem.

The pursuit of winning for one's self significantly increases our likelihood that we become selfish as we seek to protect, boost our self-esteem and avoid fear through winning, although we may or may not be aware of doing this. Without much thought we hunt for any little piece of evidence that tells us we are good enough, while, at the same time, we eagerly and proactively seek the approval from others that winning brings. We make instant judgements (generalisations or stereotypes) about someone based on their ability to win or lose. We have unconsciously learnt to see that winning is our only real option and this is grooved within our psyche at millisecond speed.

Below the surface, however, winning can be seen as a route for survival. Winning for one's self fires our natural defence system – our ego (our self-interest in survival). Our ego is our radar system monitoring any potential intruder entering our air space. If something, or someone, does enter, then our ego takes over, and Control Centre flicks the switch between fight or flight – we are constantly switched on. I have found, over the many years of working with people, that emotional turmoil is formed when we think we are either *not good enough* at something we do or that we are *rejected by others*. These represent our deepest fears. We do everything in our power to ignore them.

As a result, our ego (self-importance) is about protecting us from these two deep fears. Just as our primal instincts tell us to fight or escape, we need to fight or escape feelings of not being good enough or being rejected by others. Our ego processes this at millisecond speed but such decision-making hinders our ability to be happy and express ourselves freely.

Who, for example, can forget sitting school examinations; or taking a driving test; speaking in public; or waiting to be picked for the schools sports team? This moment is characterised by 'I win – you lose' type of thinking. We cannot change our automatic physiological stress response, where our body gets ready to fight or flee a competitive situation; but we do, however, have a choice in how our ego reacts or responds to it. We can choose a response full of fear. Here our ego is dark, selfish and focused on survival. We are filled with negative emotions like anger and fear. Alternatively, we can choose a response full of joy. Here our ego is light, selfless and focused on living to our potential. We are filled with positive emotions like joy and love.

 5. STOP: LOOK: LISTEN

Can you think of moments when you were faced with fight-or-flight choices?

What choice did you make?

What do you picture when you think you are not good enough?

What do you picture when you think of rejection?

Are you constantly switched on to things in your life, either at home, work or play?

7

An Alternative: The Masterblaster – Winning for a Community

• • •

My childhood hero was Sir Vivian Richards. I was completely absorbed by his brilliance, both technically and physically, as he would take the opposition bowling apart, and run bats-men out at will whilst fielding. It was like watching pure gold – pure athleticism. Also, he was a pioneer for the hope of a nation, who always seemed to play with a greater per-spective than just winning for oneself. For me, it was obvious that his desire to win for the people of the Caribbean was an important factor that allowed him to embrace any potential fears. He was not only an entertainer but had a huge amount of national pride and helped the people of the Caribbean feel inspired by his play on the cricket field. He had enormous charisma.

I marvelled at his presence as a player and loved it when the West Indies would come to England for the Test series so I could watch my hero. There was always something more to his play than just playing cricket. The way he went about play-ing was fascinating. He clearly showed a desire to go beyond a selfish need to win. On the surface, there was a view that he was arrogant and self-centred. However, I always looked at him from a deeper perspective in how he really wanted to do something for the community he represented. It was as if he took on the world on behalf of the downtrodden Africans who had been shipped to the Caribbean as slaves. It was clear that he felt very strongly about this. Every innings, every test series carried with it some issues of the black movement.

Sir Viv never seemed phased if things didn't go well. He always generated learning for the next time around. He saw himself in a relay race where he could pass the baton of collective excellence to the next generation. Over his immense career he was the only West Indies captain to never lose a series. He was named as Wisden's greatest ever one-day batsman, and the third best Test batsman of all time, behind Donald Bradman and Sachin Tendulkar. He was a great leader that I was to later have a chance to play against.

My chance to play against him happened towards the end of his career; he was playing county cricket and I was beginning my second year at my county. The summer was just starting and I was selected to play at Lord's against the county Sir Viv was playing for. I couldn't believe my luck. I was to play against my cricketing hero – I was beyond excited. It was such a thrill.

I can remember being in the home team changing room at Lord's. I pushed open the first door almost knowing there was a second door to go through. This second door had signage – 'Home Team Dressing Room'. As I entered, some players were sat in their allocated changing area. I stood in admiration as I recognised the distinguished names of every player who had scored a 100 or taken five wickets engraved in black ink on the honours boards up above the changing area. Sir Viv's name was proudly positioned across many years of cricket at Lord's and I was about to play against him – I could hardly believe it. The anticipation was immense.

I walked alongside this central station that housed players' lockers to the far side of the changing room. It was where I got changed ready for our usual pre-match preparation. As coaches and players started talking about the game and having banter, I couldn't help myself be drawn to the balcony to get a glimpse of the opposition making their way to the practice ground – the Nursery.

You cannot help but absorb the dense history that Lord's is filled with. Walking through the changing room doors, you're met with an oak staircase impressively housing a memorial to victims of the World Wars, leading down to the Long Room. The Long Room is internationally recognised as a vault of cricket history. Historical cricketing items, such as bats and balls in cabinets, are strategically positioned around, along with portraits and other memorabilia adorning the walls. High seated chairs are positioned either side of the double doors, looking out through the large panes of glass onto the playing area.

I walked through the MCC members' viewing area, heading to the Nursery ground for our warm ups. I opened the small white wooden gate that I'd seen so many times before on the television during Test matches, and went onto the outfield. A sense of energy can be felt emerging from the freshly cut grass, and as I closed the gate behind me I saw that Sir Viv was coming through as well. I became nervous and didn't say anything as I continued my walk across the ground to the practice area. My emotions were running high as I began to think of all those times playing in my back garden pretending I was Sir Viv and now I was here at Lord's with the man himself. Life couldn't get any better.

The coaches were already at the nets coordinating a schedule of activity that involved players doing a series of skills. Some were told to get their pads on for batting while others were told to get ready for bowling. A third group joined another coach for fielding practice. There was a buzz of excitement around the Nursery that always greeted the start of the new season. I was happy just to taste the atmosphere again and mill around chatting to both players and support staff. It was great. I was like a child on summer holidays running around having fun. We started our warm ups, but as I stretched and ran, collecting balls and throwing them to the wicketkeeper, I kept one eye trained on Sir Viv. I just couldn't help it. He was standing with a group of players hitting some catches. I just stared, feeling the enormity of being on the same pitch as the great man.

We started our bowling warm up and a group of us gathered by the nets when news filtered through that Sir Viv would not be playing as a result of a broken thumb. I was gutted. Devastated. This was always a distant dream but it was something I wanted to do – play against my hero – and it was not going to happen. I was truly sad.

As the game started, I bowled from the Pavilion End. The wicket was opposite the away team changing room. Walking back to my mark, I looked up at the balcony and there in the corner was Sir Viv. As I walked towards him I stared, with my thoughts firmly fixed on wanting to be bowling at him. Time stood still as I reflected on how important he had been in inspiring me to play cricket. As I considered this, my eyes filled and, as I blinked, tears rolled down my face. Cricket just didn't seem as important as recognising the great man's influence. I quickly wiped my eyes as I turned to bowl my next delivery.

After the day's play, I met Sir Viv in the Tavern pub, next to the ground and told him my story. He smiled and told me to keep working hard and that it would probably not have been a good idea for me to have bowled against him. I laughed – it was a great moment.

This was my start of studying world champions, like Sir Viv, at close quarters. Over the years I've had the privilege of working with them or I've been able to sit and talk to them about their sport and life in general. I have a deep passion to understand what they did. I wanted to know what the difference was. Why are they so free to express themselves under pressure?

Speaking with Sir Viv you could feel his intensity and desire to become the best and be a master – his nickname at the time was MasterBlaster. He was prepared to live for his community, both his team and his nation. This was not a self-centred act, instead he was clear on the need for self-sacrifice. Through our discussion, he was aware of his importance in inspiring others. This was amazingly complex.

He was a person who could continuously flip between self (fear) and others (joy). On the one hand, he had an overwhelming focus on self, the individual showman, enjoying putting the sword to anyone who threatened him. While on the other hand, Sir Viv had found a way to use his talent for a nation – a more selfless way of being. He understood the importance of achieving a new level of performance for the benefit of others. He understood that his real purpose in life was to serve others with what he accomplished. He made the shift from 'it's all about me winning' to 'it's all about how my winning can help others'. This way of operating is driven by joy. He would flicker between the two ways almost at will.

However, he appeared to operate with more joy than fear.

As he increased the purpose and meaning of what he was doing, he increasingly became free and happy to express himself fully. He got completely 'out of the way of himself'. The more he felt challenged by others, by being perceived as either incompetent or by being negatively judged, the more he would be free to express himself and exert a major influence on proceedings.

It became clear that world champions, like Sir Viv, are very different to the other elite athletes. I wanted to find out more. I've become passionate about understanding this at a much deeper level. I conducted lots of further research with world champion athletes, understanding why some athletes become world champions while others do not. This research was gained either by playing with or against them or in my work as a psychologist. I was interested in what made these athletes different.

 6. STOP: LOOK: LISTEN

Who was your childhood hero, and why?

How have they influenced you, and why?

What sorts of individuals inspire you?

8

Become Inspired to
Do More in Life

• • •

Sir Viv's ability to deal with adversity was an inspiration to me. Growing up watching Sir Viv was about more than just cricket; he inspired me not only with his cricketing ability but also his instinct for justice and fairness. It was fascinating to watch him deal with adversity with his immense talent. The more verbal abuse from opponents he received, the more his resolve to use cricket to come out on top deepened. The level of hostility toward him, his team and country made him even more determined to succeed. This was great to watch; here was a man who was clearly hell-bent on showcasing that his people would have the last laugh.

He was fervently opposed to the policy of apartheid in South Africa and turned down money, wealth and fame to go on a cricket tour to that country – another illustration of his great strength of character. He played the game based on his values and beliefs, which simply could not be compromised. I became transfixed by his ability to respond to adversity and from this early age it helped me to deal with hardship growing up.

7. STOP: LOOK: LISTEN

What values and standards will you not compromise in life?

Who displays similar standards and values as you?

What circumstances will lead you to sacrifice your values and standards?

9

Learning to Deal with Adversity

• • •

While I dreamt of playing first class cricket, as a mixed-race boy growing up in leafy Home Counties I was taken aback by the negative judgement of me by others. I couldn't understand why people were so harsh simply due to the colour of my skin. I didn't know it then but I was developing a thirst for understanding what the deeper underlying causes were for such negativity, prejudice and discrimination. Today, this is commonly known as 'unconscious bias'. As a child I would regularly wonder what life was all about and increasingly became interested in how others automatically perceived me before they had a chance to know me.

My brother and I were among the few mixed-race children in the town. At school, teachers, pupils and parents treated us differently, which I found hard because all I wanted was to feel like I belonged. I was loved and accepted by my parents but felt alienated by a school system that took no time to understand me, or my cultural differences. I would regularly be upset and complain to my parents; although always supportive and caring, my father's view was to urge us to brush ourselves down, get on with it, and establish ways to develop our lives. He spent time helping us understand that the only solution to the harsh reality of prejudice was to excel in whatever we did, whether it was through sport or education. He saw our education as the key to gaining independence.

When I entered my teens, I was taken to St Vincent, my father's homeland in the West Indies. This holiday was a real eye-opener, and gave me much-needed perspective. It felt like a home away from home, and I established some strong roots in my identity, being able to appreciate a new sense of belonging from my extended family in the Caribbean. It was a real tonic to coping with the realities of school in England. I felt life had been pumped into me, just as giving water to a plant ensures its survival.

My father's belief in the value of education was second to none. He was a proud hard-working man, who'd worked as a machinist for over thirty years in a local furniture company. He felt his work options were limited due to the lack of formal education he had received back in the Caribbean. This meant that he had little choice in doing anything else, but this didn't stop his eagerness to encourage his children. He fervently wanted more for his sons and he made us pay attention to our education; he felt this was the only response to the experience of prejudice or unconscious bias. He would constantly reinforce this due to his strong desire that we develop our lives, careers and opportunities beyond him. His unwavering support shone through all the negativity from others in life as he pushed us to achieve more and more both in sport and education. Not surprisingly, my interest in how I saw myself led to the subject of psychology.

8. STOP: LOOK: LISTEN

What was life like for you growing up?

What are your relationships like with your parents and/or your siblings?

What was your school life like?

What is the relationship like with your father or father figure?

How do you deal with adversity in life?

Have you ever negatively judged someone on first impressions?

Do you know what your taken-for-granted attitudes and behaviours (unconscious bias) are?

10

Studying Psychology

• • •

When I started 'A' level psychology I fell in love with the subject. I was fascinated with the concept of negative stereotyping and I conducted a cross-cultural study on the self-esteem of primary school children in St Vincent in the West Indies compared with school children from Vincentian background but born in Britain. I explored the different mind-set of culturally similar people growing up in different countries.

At Goldsmith's College, University of London, I studied psychology at degree level, where I conducted another cross-cultural study looking at the level of role stress for constables and sergeants in the Metropolitan police force compared with those in the St Vincent police force. I was fascinated to see the similarities and differences in the level of stress experienced by police officers doing very different types of policing, but holding the same organisational position. Here the very different systems engendered very different thinking.

I then took a master's in occupational and organisational psychology at the University of East London, where my research focused on investigating a firm of fund managers in the City of London. My aim was to understand the basic taken-for-granted assumptions of the organisation and the automatic behaviour staff chose – that is, their unconscious bias. I wanted to understand the leadership's impact on the organisational culture, and ultimately its performance.

I carried out in-depth interviews about how people operated within the organisation, and spent time either observing behaviour in meetings or conducting group discussion in order to hear what staff were feeling and thinking, so collecting data from all levels of the organisation. I found getting a deeper appreciation of the underlying psychology of individuals and groups became important to me; the in-depth interviews enabled me to truly understand taken-for-granted assumptions, attitudes, behaviours, values and beliefs. Discussion groups became a way of sharing thoughts about what people were seeing and experiencing. In all my research and work I've collected important information by trying to understand each person or each team and their real issues and pains, their meaning and purpose. I found I could better understand the people I was investigating by getting a more in-depth look at them, but also by collaborating *with* them to establish their context or perspective, experiences and perceptions. It was research *with-the-subject* and not research *on-the-subject*, where people have the opportunity to construct their thinking in their own way using their own words.

 9. STOP: LOOK: LISTEN

What do you love doing in life?

How often do you get to do what you love in life?

What stops you from doing what you love in life?

One of my early experiences of applied psychology was whilst playing professional cricket. I became excited when an eminent sport psychologist came in to run a team workshop. I thought this would be a perfect opportunity for me to combine my interest in psychology with my time at my second county. However, along with most of the team, including some well-known international players, I found it a fruitless exercise.

The psychologist conducted the session as if he were a teacher standing in front of his class, imparting his knowledge and expertise to his silent and attentive students. We were nothing more than passive recipients; we were given questionnaires to complete, following which he gave a presentation, citing some studies. I didn't feel a part of his presentation and the content didn't match my expectations regarding how psychology can help me in performing more consistently. He presented a top-down or a command and control approach which was totally misaligned to what I wanted and needed as a player; I believed that if I was active in the process, then I was more likely to adopt some new ideas, and this was clearly not happening. I wanted him to listen to me and help me establish ways of making the best of my ability after being released from my first county, but instead I switched off to his exercises and questionnaires, as did many of the players. We all had the feeling that we were just there to be a part of his research. I left feeling quite dejected by what sport psychology could offer. This was further reinforced when I tried to use sport psychology techniques to help me produce winning performances.

I had bought all the latest texts on sport psychology interventions in an attempt to use the techniques, proven in science, to improve my consistency. I assumed that given my experience as a postgraduate student in psychology I would readily adopt these new methods to help my performance. I went through a range of interventions, from relaxation and guided visualisation techniques, to performance coping strategies, to goal-setting, to a whole host of other methods for peak performance. The results were paradoxical. On the one hand, these techniques were the latest strategies to help develop high performance, while on the other, I was not consistently improving by using them. My performances were still riddled with inconsistency. Why? Was it me or was there something else going on?

Over the last twenty years I have come to realise that sport psychology interventions are not the most effective way of helping elite athletes deliver peak performance; they are best delivered to young athletes starting out in their sporting endeavour as, for some reason, the delivery of expert knowledge to elite athletes didn't translate. It didn't work for me as a participant and it didn't work for me as a consultant trying to help elite athletes achieve more. In my early days of consulting, elite athletes would enjoy the fact that they were going to hear from a sport psychologist – they also had read all the books.

However, I took a very different approach with them, which they found very refreshing. They took full participation in finding a solution to their own performance inconsistency, making them fully engaged and responsive to finding their own solutions. On each occasion I would act as an outside change agent to the sport highlighting to both the coaches and athletes contradictions and conflicts regarding the delivery of high performance. These early consultancy experiences confirmed my plan was impactful and significant, as the clients felt fully involved in finding a solution to their performance problems.

I started consulting with British Diving and specifically working with a number of female divers in their preparation for the upcoming Olympic Games. I also consulted with GB Athletics sprinters as well as the British Tennis Foundation, Great Britain Orienteering and the World Snooker Association.

 10. STOP: LOOK: LISTEN

What experiences have you had where you expected one thing but received something quite different?

How did that make you feel – disappointed? Challenged? Energised?

What did you do next?

How do you cope with not getting what you want?

PART THREE
The World Champion Discovery

11

World Champion Athletes' Results

· · ·

What I learned from working with world champions and elite athletes was the opposite of what I'd expected to find:

Elite athletes who became world champions were selfless at the moment of crossing the line to become the best in the world.

Does this sound to you like a contradiction? It does to me. But that doesn't worry me; over the last twenty years or so, as a professional sportsman and chartered psychologist, son, brother, husband, father, uncle and friend, I have come to the view that I'm truly filled with many contradictions. That is, saying one thing but doing the opposite. Here are a few statements in my cricket career that illustrate the difference between what I've said compared to what I've done:

* I'm in control of something when I'm clearly out of control *e.g. I tried to control how many runs are scored off my final ball when as soon as I release the ball the batsman's determined where he will hit it.*
* I believe in myself but I'm constantly looking for evidence that I'm good enough *e.g. I know I've given my*

best performance but I'm eager to get proof from my captain and coach that I was good enough.

- I strived to win at something important but instead experienced losing *e.g. I captained my university cricket team to the London University Cup Final that we subsequently lost.*
- It's all about my team winning but really it is about me winning *e.g. I'm disappointed we lost but I was happy with my own performance.*
- I tried to avoid making mistakes but errors stuck to me like a bad smell *e.g. The harder I tried to avoid bowling poor deliveries the more I made them.*
- I desperately wanted to make more time for my family and friends but I experience giving no time to them *e.g. I became so consumed by my game that I stopped spending time with others.*
- I try to put the effort into being consistent but end up showing others one thing and feeling another *e.g. I tried to bowl with consistency but continued to feel frustrated with my performance.*
- I am keen to have fun but I actually feel miserable at times *e.g. I enjoyed having fun playing cricket but the strains of professional cricket made me, at times, feel miserable.*
- I want to genuinely help others but I end up simply taking from others *e.g. I regularly talked about supporting others with their game but I was eager to enlist others to help me.*
- I thought my purpose was to play cricket but felt confused when my first county released me *e.g. I dreamed of playing international cricket when in reality I retired at an early age.*

11. STOP: LOOK: LISTEN

Does any of this sound familiar to you?

What is the solution?

What times can you think of when you were filled with conflict and contradiction?

How do you normally deal with contradiction in your life?

My work with elite athletes and world champions found that there was a better way of dealing with our contradictions or paradoxes in life. These elite athletes and world champions soon realised that it wasn't the contradictions that were the problem, but what they told themselves as they reacted to them. By helping them understand this shift, they were able to see more clearly 'what they told themselves' – their ego, or level of selfishness, was the problem especially when approaching that crossing the line moment. Their response was to reduce their self-importance and increase their selflessness. That is, they cultivated their awareness of how others could benefit from their achievements instead of being completely self-absorbed by what was in it for them by winning. They learnt that reducing self-importance was the most effective way of dealing with their conflict or contradictions. Or, to put it another way, their leadership in dealing with ambiguity or unclear situations/outcomes meant that they chose to be selfless, under the most extreme pressure, which helped them cope with the contradictions better.

This book aims to help you examine your contradictions better. That is, when what you say (or don't say) clashes with your experience (e.g. you state your desire to win but instead you experience losing). As stated in earlier sections of the book, you can only improve and change something if you are committed and willing to examine your conflicts and contradictions.

12

The Myth of the World Champion
– a Contradiction Confirmed

• • •

 12. STOP: LOOK: LISTEN

The contradiction being:

Becoming the best in the world can help others.

What do you think of this?

My assumption about reaching the top in my sport was wrong. It was clear that my unconscious bias around the traditional attributes associated with reaching the top – a selfish ruthless obsession with winning – was not helpful in crossing the line at world championship level. I found that these were not the abiding characteristics that enabled an individual (or team) to be free to express their skills, especially under pressure. Instead, I found being *selfless* was more effective in sustaining high-level performance. I was truly shocked and surprised by these findings. They felt wrong, because they were the opposite of what I'd been striving for all my life. They seemed completely counter-intuitive; perhaps even revolutionary. World Champion athletes didn't think as I expected them to do.

I became passionate about understanding this at a much deeper level, conducting further qualitative research with world champion athletes as to how they were able to choose a selfless mind-set under the most intense pressure. These elite athletes became acutely aware that the mind-set that took them to world-class level was inadequate for becoming the best in the world. They let go of being self-absorbed in their pursuit of winning and moved to a more value-based mind-set about the deeper purpose of becoming a world champion. Some considered how their success could positively impact people; be it individuals, communities or even nations, while others simply chose a selfless state due to catastrophic stress experienced by the pursuit of winning a world championship. Regardless of whether they, wittingly or unwittingly, knew they had chosen such a mind-set, I could immediately see them become much more open and free, as if a heavy weight had been lifted off their shoulders. It was amazing to watch and experience these athletes significantly improve their ability to perform. It was also fascinating to see their complete shock and euphoria as they crossed the line to achieve their lifetime's dream. Winning stunned them.

They found a deeper set of attitudes, behaviours, values and beliefs for relishing the mastery of their task that went beyond just the desire to win. They became free to express themselves. They got completely *out of the way of themselves*. Their normal fear of judgement, rejection and humiliation had gone for that moment while they were fully immersed in the execution of their task. During this intense period their automatic taken-for-granted high level of self-importance was replaced with a deep sense of perspective – 'achieving this can't just be for me'. They had found a purpose, a personal meaning that went beyond them.

Moreover, they had a deeper appreciation of what they were doing. They began developing the notion of being a part of something much bigger than themselves. In contrast, however, other elite athletes who fell short of becoming the best in the world got very defensive, and were unwilling to make this shift with any real meaning and personal truth. They simply couldn't let go of their self-importance. They were rigidly stuck in a self-absorbed state – always finding an excuse for everything. It made me realise how damaging my total single-mindedness had been whilst chasing my own dream, something my father tried to point out when he referred to me as 'wanting it too much'. I now had the evidence and the privilege of witnessing several individuals becoming the best in the world through choosing a without ego or selfless mind-set and my findings were now obvious. I began thinking: what if you could apply these findings to everyone?

 13. STOP: LOOK: LISTEN

What impact would it have if we all pursued winning from a selfless perspective?

World Champion athletes realised their execution of skills required something different. They were no longer just good athletes, they appreciated they were entering a new stage. It was as if they understood they were about to get to the summit of the biggest mountain in the world. They appreciated being at the altitude required a new way of climbing compared to their initial ascent into world class standard. The thinner air meant they had to take each step as carefully as they could whilst also thinking about the welfare of others. Here time appeared to stand still as they ensured the safety of not only themselves but also their team. They accepted they were not in control at this level and having a selfish, ruthless obsession with getting to the top didn't serve them well at altitude. Instead, they chose greater flexibility in letting go of '*control*'. This is difficult, as control is one of the key attributes necessary for becoming world class. This acceptance over not being in control led them to become the best in the world. Such a transformation is a difficult and special feat. As a result, all the selfishness needed to ascend the highest mountain towards their ultimate dream had, for a short time (or longer), disappeared. Getting to the summit, or achieving their dreams, required thinking of others whilst *sipping* the air very gently and masterfully.

In conclusion, this paradox between striving for individual success whilst appreciating the importance of serving others was termed the *World Champion Contradiction*. The evidence was compelling. On the one hand, you can choose to be selfish – focussing on winning for oneself. Here you become tough, closed and individually focussed in pursuit of success for yourself. Your focus is on extrinsic rewards: wealth, fame and recognition are all seen and experienced on the surface, leading to *performance inconsistency and poor mental health*.

On the other hand, however, you can choose to be selfless – focussed on winning for your team or community. Here you become softer, more open and serve others while in pursuit of success. Your focus is on intrinsic rewards: freedom, happiness and purpose are all unseen and experienced below the surface, leading to *performance consistency and good mental health*. I found that a world champion who is focused on winning for oneself never appears satisfied with winning – winning is never enough! In contrast, a world champion in pursuit of winning for the benefit of others first appears happier, more fulfilled and on purpose. They transcend winning and losing. They accept that selfishness and selflessness are two sides of the same coin. Flip it one way you are **selfish**, flip it the other way you are **selfless**. This deeper type of thinking led to questions regarding who they are and what was their purpose in life.

I saw that if you choose a selfless response you are going in the right direction. This means your 'ego' or 'what you tell yourselves' is quiet. You become totally immersed in the pursuit of a task for the genuine contribution you can make to your team or community. This is the human delight and real purpose you receive when you serve others through winning. Here you are totally out of the way of yourselves as you learn to appreciate there is a much bigger goal than simply winning for oneself. It is characterised by the question: *what can my success do to contribute to my community; be it team, family, or wider society first?* In being able to answer this question, you naturally discover what your purpose in life is. I have discovered much greater joy when I serve others and go beyond winning or losing. I was amazed that I experienced greater euphoria when a snooker player, GB Orienteer and a GB Kickboxer I was supporting became world champions than achieving my own dream of running out at Lord's to play cricket. Such athletes make a significant shift from *'it's all about me winning'* to *'it's all about how my winning can help others'*. As they increased the purpose and meaning of what they were doing, they increasingly became free and happy to express themselves fully.

 14. STOP: LOOK: LISTEN

Are you stopped in your tracks by the notion that your ego may be one of the biggest reasons behind you not fulfilling your potential?

Are you willing and committed to stop, look and listen to your ego when in pursuit of winning in life?

Are you able to *get out of the way of yourself* when you are doing something important?

Can you choose when to let go of your selfishness when you are under pressure?

13

Flipping a Coin

• • •

I spoke at a prestigious golf event with a golfer who said, 'It's all about *me* winning,' meaning as an individual, while the best performances of his life have ironically come in team events such as the Ryder Cup.

We all have the ability to form an instant opinion on something, and in millisecond speed, to take a completely different view of the same thing. We are very adept at holding two completely different views at the same time. What is the benefit of doing this? It gives us more choice to select what we feel is the most appropriate response to any situation we are presented with. In this example, the golfer uses what he tells himself to explain both his individual and team success.

I liken it to the two sides of the same coin; flip it one way, and you can choose a focus on individual excellence; or, alternatively, flip it the other way and you can have a concentration on team excellence.

These are two mutually exclusive opposites – two competing forces for our attention. We operate as if we have a coin in our hands, ready to toss it and see which side it lands on. We can flip it one way and we are dark and selfish, choosing negative emotions like anger to avoid experiencing our deepest fears. Or we can flip it the other way and we are selfless, choosing emotions like joy to embrace our deepest fears. Whether we are aware of it or not, we choose which side our coin lands when we are doing something important – either dark, selfish and fearful or light, selfless and joyful.

Let's not forget, though, that we are clever beings; our ego is there by design – it is there for a reason. It has evolved for the purposes of self-interest, self-protection and survival. Importantly, it is not there for self-care. In this context, our ego protects us from our fear.

For example, when we are doing something important, thoughts about whether we are going to win or lose flood our minds. This is our 'ego' talking to us. That is, our ego comes alive through what we say when we are about to do something important. I'm sure you can remember the thoughts and feelings you had when going for a job interview or giving a presentation at work. Regardless of whether we make a positive or negative statement, what we tell ourselves has some survival interest at its heart. There is a distinct pay-off or benefit for saying whatever we say about ourselves, whether we are aware of it or not.

If we choose the dark and selfish response we are going in the wrong direction. This means our 'ego' or 'what we tell ourselves' flies in to help us cope with the feeling of being out of control. Our sole concern is to survive the stressful situation we are in. Here, our ego protects us from meltdown: *'I'm not sure if I want to do this anyway; or it doesn't really matter what happens; or what if I lose? What will others think of me? I don't think I'm good enough anyway.'* These statements and questions illustrate a selfish act, as we attempt to survive the win-lose situation we find ourselves in. We are results-focused; if we win we survive our thoughts – like a stay of execution. If we lose, however, our thoughts or 'ego' spirals out of control as we try to make sense of the mismatch between what we expect and the outcome. We send ourselves into complete distress.

 15. STOP: LOOK: LISTEN

Understanding your own ego is key to your freedom, happiness and success.

Your ego reflects your attitude, behaviour values and beliefs in life.

Essentially you will be able to see *what you tell yourself* impacts how you behave under stress.

You will be able to see how your values and beliefs impact your behaviour and how your behaviour impacts your ego.

This process is the start of being able to *get out the way* of yourself.

PART FOUR

How to Detox Your Ego

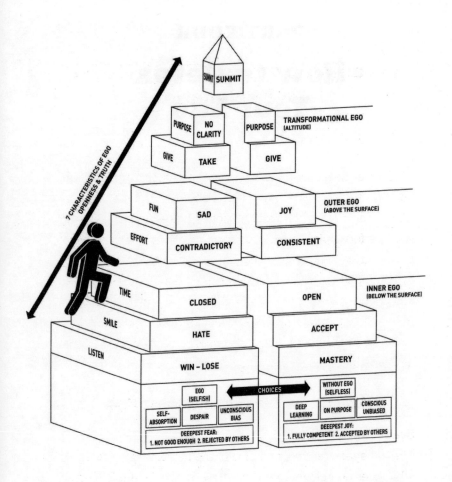

Leadership withoutEGO® Model

14

Leadership withoutEGO® Model – an Explanation

• • •

There are three stages to ego: the inner ego, the outer ego, and the transformational ego. To begin to understand any underlying motivations and anxieties you experience during your performance, you need to be aware of each of these; once you become aware of them, you have the opportunity to correct them. By asking yourself seven key questions as you progress through each stage, you can identify where you lie on the continuum with selfishness at one end and self-lessness at the other. The Leadership withoutEGO® Model demonstrates this further.

The Seven Characteristics of Ego

Stage One. Inner Ego

The 'inner ego' is the first stage of the process and it refers to what goes on below the surface. This is what you tell yourself that no one sees. It consists of the first three characteristics on the Leadership withoutEGO® Model: **Listen**, **Smile** and **Time**.

- *Step One: Listen*
  How much do you want to win for yourself compared to winning for others?

This is the first and most important question of your ego detox. Here you are invited to listen to whether you want to win for yourself or win for others. If you take a winning for yourself attitude you are choosing a 'win-lose' mind-set. This increases your stress reaction, lack of freedom and your ability to execute under pressure. If however, you take a winning for others attitude you are choosing a 'mastery' mind-set.

If you choose an 'I'm a winner' or 'I'm a loser' (win-lose) way of thinking in your life, you are picking an ego reaction. This is paying attention to fear in your life and is characterised by the statement: *'I always want to win for myself.'* A reaction like this means you are in fact triggering your ego. Focusing on winning for yourself means you will limit your freedom, happiness and success. However, if you are immersed in the mastery of your skills, you are choosing a selfless response, as you understand how the delivery of your skills supports your team or community. You will pay attention to joy in your life. This takes courage and is characterised by the statement: *'I always want to be the best I can be.'*

- ### *Step Two: Smile*
Do you smile at your errors?
After completing Step One, you are now invited to explore whether you smile at your errors in life. You need to be aware as to whether you 'hate your errors' or 'love your errors'. If you choose to hate your errors in life, you are choosing an ego reaction. This is characterised by the statement: *'I hate making mistakes.'* If you have a reaction like this, you are in fact ignoring great learning

in your life. A hatred for errors means you will limit your freedom, happiness and success. However, if you are open to generating learning from your errors, you are choosing a selfless response as you begin to find a way to be even more helpful to your community. This can be characterised by the statement: *'I am fully open and alert to learning from my mistakes.'*

- ## Step Three: Time

  Do you take time to consider what you avoid?
  Following the completion of Steps One and Two, you will have important data on what choices you make in your pursuit of winning. For example, do you take a win-lose mind-set when you are doing something important? Or do you have a negative emotional reaction to errors? This third step is about taking time to explore what you avoid when pursuing something important. Are you willing and committed to taking the time to explore what you avoid? You will either choose either a 'closed' or 'open' mind-set. For example, are you open or closed to the questions asked so far? If you are closed to looking at avoidance in your life, you are choosing an ego reaction. This is characterised by the statement: *'I don't really avoid anything.'* Clearly, such a reaction means you are in fact avoiding some uncomfortable truths and by being closed, you will limit your freedom, happiness and success in life. However, if you are open to what you avoid, you are choosing a selfless response as you begin to find a way to be even more helpful to your community. You are choosing to pay attention to joy in your life. This takes courage and is characterised

by the statement: *'I am open to all things, even though it is difficult and uncomfortable to talk about.'*

Stage Two. Outer Ego

The next stage you must now pay attention to is your 'outer ego'. This is what is seen above the surface. Your outer ego is what you tell yourself that's seen by others when you are doing something important. It consists of the next two characteristics of the Leadership withoutEGO® Model: **Effort** and **Fun**.

- *Step Four: Effort*

  Do you deliver what you say and feel?

  Do you put the effort in to closing the gap between what you feel and what you do? Here you need to develop the ability to tolerate ambiguity in your life. Do others see you having a 'consistent' or a 'say one thing – do another' mind-set? Here you will either show consistency or inconsistency in your attitudes, behaviour, values and beliefs. If you choose to be inconsistent, you are choosing an ego reaction. This is characterised by the statement: *'I experience separation between what I feel and what I show.'* This means that in fact you are being inconsistent in how you do things. Such separation means you will limit your freedom, happiness and success. However, if you are open to understanding your level of consistency, you are choosing a selfless response as you begin to find a way to be even more helpful to your community. You are choosing to pay attention to joy in your life. This takes courage and is characterised by the statement: *'I do what I say and mean.'*

- ### *Step Five: Fun*

  Do you have fun?

  The next characteristic of your outer ego is your decision to either have fun or feel miserable in what you do. This decision will mean you either show joy in whatever you do or appear unhappy with whatever you do. If you choose to not have fun in your life, you are choosing an ego reaction. You are subsequently choosing to pay attention to fear in your life. This is characterised by the statement: *'I am sad and emotionless when I'm performing.'* Such sadness means you will limit your freedom, happiness and success. However, if you are open to having fun, you are choosing a selfless response as you begin to find a way to be even more helpful to your community. You are choosing to pay attention to joy in your life. This takes courage and is characterised by the statement: *'I see the humour in difficult situations.'*

Stage Three. Transformational Ego

After you have considered these steps dealing with your inner and outer ego, you must now focus on how you can apply this learning to influence and inspire others: your transformational ego. Here the person has genuine care and empathy for others, putting others first. They create an environment with a focus on the collective excellence of the team or community. In addition, they feel total competence with their skills and are freely capable of calling on others for help. They don't need recognition from others. They are able to **give** to others and gain feedback on what their **purpose** in life is.

- ### *Step Six: Give*

Do you give to others?

When you set out to do something important do you have a 'give' or 'take' mind-set? Is your main focus on how it will benefit you or do you consider how what you do can help others? If you choose not to give in your life, you are choosing an ego reaction. You are choosing to bring fear in your life. This is characterised by the statement: *'I don't get what I want from others.'* Taking from others means you will limit your freedom, happiness and success in life. However, if you are open to understanding your level of giving, you are choosing a selfless response as you begin to find a way to be even more helpful to your community. You are choosing to pay attention to and bring joy to your life. This takes courage and is characterised by the statement: *'I am happy to give to others.'*

- ### *Step Seven: Purpose*

What is your purpose?

The final step in this process of transformational ego asks you to consider whether you have a 'purpose' to what you do or 'no purpose' at all. Do you know what direction you're heading in or do you lack a sense of meaning in what you do? If you choose not to have clarity of direction in your life, you are choosing an ego reaction. This is a fearful response and is characterised by the statement: *'I do not know what my purpose in life is.'* Having no direction means you will limit your freedom, happiness and success in life. However, if you are open to understanding your purpose, you are choosing a selfless response as you begin to find a way to be even more helpful to your community. This shows an awareness of joy in your life. This takes courage and is characterised by the statement: *'I know what my purpose in life is.'*

In Conclusion: Reaching the Summit

After progressing through these three stages you will have a deep sense of understanding as to how you operate under pressure. By working through the Seven Steps, you will be in a better position to understand the elements of your inner and outer ego. Such clarity will allow you to develop your Transformational ego. This is key to performing with freedom and happiness.

In my experience with elite athletes when they were approaching the finishing line to become world champions, I discovered that, for various reasons, reaching the summit triggered a significant shift from self-absorption to a selfless state. That is, instead of being self-centred, they became aware of how winning could benefit others. This was a counterintuitive finding that indicated the importance of serving others at the heart of what you do when you are doing something important.

Consequently, if you want to take the journey to the summit of the Leadership withoutEGO® Model for yourself, you must also make a shift in your mind-set, like the world champions. Here the world champion is like a climber exposed to lower oxygen levels at higher altitude on a mountain. He or she needs to constantly be aware of what they must do in order to ensure the safety of themselves and their team members. Similarly you will need to lower ego levels in order to advance. So you must pay great attention to what your ego tells you. The seven questions across the three stages enable you to detox your ego. The hardest stage for a climber is coping with the drop in oxygen levels near the top of their ascent. For someone progressing up the Leadership withoutEGO® Model, their hardest stage is transforming their ego so that they place the needs of others first (operate without ego) and as a result reach the summit to experience freedom, happiness and success.

When you are open you enter a world of deep learning through being consciously unbiased (effortless). So, in millisecond speed, you have two leadership choices available to you.

Leadership Choice 1:

LISTEN to how winning and losing impact on you. When you pursue mastery of something it allows you to move away from ego (i.e. a without ego approach). You are automatically free to express yourself and you feel totally competent and accepted by others in all you do. You will examine how to become even more expert at what you do and see winning and losing as routes to greater mastery of your skills.

As a result, you will **SMILE** at your errors. You will love the deep learning gained from your errors. You will be in an appreciative mode over the learning generated from errors. You will take **TIME** to unravel what you avoid. You will put **EFFORT** into understanding the difference between how you feel and what you experience. You will see your personal truth and naturally align and self-correct your thinking with what's happening when you are doing something important. Such deep alignment leads to greater satisfaction as you begin to have more **FUN** with what you do. Even though you may feel out of control regarding the result of your performance, you strangely feel alright with what is about to happen as you generate as much learning as possible through the execution of your task. You feel in complete control even though you are out of control.

This is similar to being 'in the zone'. You are effortless or consciously unbiased about what you tell yourself which only heightens your ability to make the right decisions at the right time regarding what you do. You are happy and begin to **GIVE** more to those around you, as you feel responsible for using your performance to serve others. The way you perform inspires others to follow. You begin to feel immense satisfaction as others truly benefit from the way you perform and live. It is the positive feedback of others that gives clarity to your true **PURPOSE** in life. You feel you are living a good and fulfilled life.

You become flexible and open to the real truth underlying who you are and what you are doing. You unravel the reality about your situation – avoiding nothing. You see your real uncomfortable truth. As a result, you love your errors as they are seen in a totally positive light. You feel alignment between your feelings and reality. Such consistency results in feeling happy with what you are doing. More often than not, this leads to attributing the right causes for poor performance. You know this but you choose to learn from it. Such freedom leads to a joyful appearance when you are performing.

Leadership Choice 2:

In contrast, when you pursue beating other people at something it triggers your ego. You automatically go into survival mode in order to protect yourself from your deepest fears of either not being good enough or feeling rejected by others. Your ego attempts to protect you from such fears using three critical facets – self-absorption, despair and unconscious bias. All of which distract you from your deepest fears. So, in millisecond speed, you will begin to think about what impact losing will have on you.

Such self-centredness only leads to despair. You panic and choke as you unwittingly consider the consequences of losing. What you tell yourself immediately interferes and slows your decision-making down. This results in inconsistency in performance, and steers your unconscious bias so that you become rigid and closed to what the real truth is underlying losing to someone else. You avoid processing the reality about your situation. You are blind to your real uncomfortable truth.

As a result, you hate making errors as they are seen in a totally negative light. You feel tension between your feelings and reality. Such a contradiction results in you finding ways to explain your inconsistency. More often than not, this leads to attributing the wrong causes for poor performance. You know this but you choose to ignore it. Such hidden tension leads to a miserable appearance when you are performing. You look sad and begin to demand more from others as you wrestle with the stress of not performing optimally. This leads to a lack of clarity about what your inconsistent performances mean in your life. While some of your performances lead to success, you don't feel satisfied with your achievements. You feel empty and unfulfilled.

STOP **16. STOP: LOOK: LISTEN**

What did you think of the Leadership withoutEGO® Model?

What choice do you make most often – selfish or selfless?

15

The Leadership withoutEGO®
Model – Awareness, Belief and
Correction Plan (ABC Plan)

• • •

The seven characteristics of the ego are as pictured here:
listen, smile, time, effort, fun, give and **purpose**.

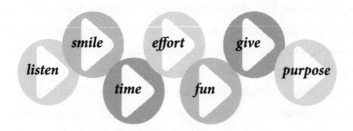

Having a lack of awareness in one, some or all of these characteristics leads to unhappiness, restriction and significant stress. The truth is, pursuing winning for one's self encourages us to become narrow, rigid and tough. As a result, you become inflexible across the seven characteristics outlined above. You become closed and choose negative emotions to help you beat your opponent. Consequently, you will tend to ignore and bury things you perceive as potentially painful, like losing.

This is bad.

We shouldn't do this but it is a natural, automatic response to perceived fear. In so doing, you will hinder your chances of sustaining true happiness, freedom and success. You will be in no position to deliver high performance. You become blind to the fact that *what you tell yourself* (your ego) will attempt to protect you from perceived danger or conflict by ensuring you pay no attention to these characteristics. In essence, your ego prevents you from being open to seeing what you fear; this is the uncomfortable truth about how we choose to live and perform. The invitation for you is to unravel and understand your ego by working through the seven characteristics, or Seven Steps.

The Seven Steps will be outlined in more detail so that you can discover how to build your own ABC Plan using your inner, outer and transformational ego when you are doing something important. Here you will discover what step is most relevant to you and where you need to increase awareness, develop belief and make corrections.

As you read through each step, I would like to invite you to develop your own Awareness, Belief and Correction (ABC) Plan. It is necessary to have your ABC Plan in the back of your mind as I share experiences and stories within each of the Seven Steps. My aim is to help you reflect on your own experiences as you begin to process the examples given.

You will be required to stop, look and listen to your own internal traffic regarding each of the seven characteristics of ego in your life. Each step may or may not surprise you, or it may even trigger a certain amount of fear. You will need to be willing and committed to becoming more open with what you tell yourself, what choices you make and what your own personal truth is. I typically impress upon someone the power of slowing down and processing thoughts, feelings and action in this way.

Your selfishness needs to be assessed and stopped in order to truly begin the process of self-discovery. You may unwittingly avoid uncomfortable thoughts, feelings or things. You may hold high expectations regarding winning or hate making mistakes. You may say one thing but do another and be unhappy with your lot. You may take from others or spend no time reflecting on what you do. All of these are ego led and a bad situation for us – they all require change.

 17. STOP: LOOK: LISTEN

What is your immediate impression of the seven characteristics of ego?

Are you prepared to stop, look and listen to your own internal traffic regarding each of the seven characteristics of ego?

If you are not, this is your ego talking.

You must learn to consider '*what you tell yourself*' so that you can learn how to embrace all seven characteristics if gains are to be made.

Your journey starts with awareness of your attitude to things in your life. This is unseen by you and others. You will then be invited to consider assessing your behaviour, which is observed by everyone. Finally, you will be asked to think deeply about your strongly held values and beliefs that direct both your attitudes and behaviours. These are below the surface, buried as if they are in the hull of a ship. Also below the surface are two of our deepest fears, that we are either *'not good enough'* or that we will be *'rejected by others'*.

These two fears act as if they are a rudder controlling and driving which journey and what direction we take. If unnoticed and unchecked, they have a massive negative influence on us as they try to protect us from feeling vulnerable and exposed. They are responsible for enabling us to bury the emotional pain we experience our lives.

However, our emotional blockages do surface through our ego – our ego is a window into our emotional pain and blockages. On the one hand, we try to protect and hide our fears from ourselves, while on the other hand, they manifest within us as what we tell ourselves. By assessing what we tell ourselves we can begin to explore these two fears more deeply.

The seven characteristics of ego we've already encountered act as if they are our DNA, telling us which journey and direction to take. Each of us has a unique blend of the seven characteristics that we need to understand; each one can influence us to varying degrees and it will take you some time to become aware, believe and correct your very own ego DNA pattern.

The method to establish your ego pattern is the ABC Plan. This ABC process is similar to the ABC in first aid: Awareness replaces Airway, Belief replaces Breathing and Correction replaces Circulation. If you choose to follow the ABC process, it will be like putting yourself in the recovery position as if you were administering ABC first aid to yourself.

You will feel more joy and freedom as you begin to explore each of the Seven Steps; it will be a hard and difficult process, but the rewards will be life-changing. This ABC process is essential in learning how to operate without ego or selflessly. It will change how you experience your life and requires complete commitment and time so that you can assess and develop a plan to shift your view on each of the characteristics of ego in order to improve your life.

The seven characteristics are interconnected and interdependent on each other. As a result, working through the first step – Listen – allows you to understand your attitude to winning, which leads you to the second step: Smile. Being able to smile at your errors leads you to the third step: Time. Taking time to understand what you avoid leads to the fourth step: Effort. Putting effort into understanding your inconsistencies leads to the fifth step: Fun. Being able to have fun leads to the sixth step: Give. Being able to give to others leads to the seventh step: Purpose. Learning to understand your purpose through how you serve others transforms your ego and you reach the summit.

Working through the Seven Steps will enable you to shift from winning for yourself to winning for others. This will give you greater purpose, as you will see the benefit of operating without ego in your life. You will shift from a selfish to a selfless perspective. You will be better positioned to understand your underlying values and beliefs that you hold. You will be keen to align your attitudes and behaviours to a newly found insight about your values and beliefs. You will become happier, freer and more successful with what you do.

Constructing your own ABC Plan means you will be in a better position to see how each step highlights the impact of your ego. In this way, you will begin to truly assess what you do when you are doing something important. You will be able to align your dreams and fears in life with your attitude, behaviour, core values and beliefs. You will feel happier understanding that your automatic ego response to wanting to win for oneself may not be advantageous; you will understand that this will trigger fear as thoughts of losing and what it means flood your mind. You begin to think of the fears of not being good enough and not getting the support from others. Understanding how our fears trigger our ego is key. You need to see it, embrace it and celebrate it if you are to conquer your deep-seated fears and achieve your dreams and live a fulfilled life.

Taking time to work through each of the seven characteristics of ego will help you become free to perform when it matters the most to you in life. You will be better able to execute a skill or task with greater ease. There will be a great appreciation of the context in which you are performing. You will have clarity about how to perform your task regardless of the situation.

As you pursue winning with the aim of it benefiting others, you will accept that you may feel a lack of control at times. You will see mistakes as a route to learning and improvement. You will be free of your deepest fears of not being good enough and being rejected by others. You will choose a world where there will be no threat, restriction or judgement from others. You will gain insight into what drives you and learn how to discover a spiritual dimension to your life. You will have childlike, joyous abandonment and express yourself with total freedom and fun. You will have a free mind. There will be no tension, anxiety or stress and you will be able to make the right decisions at the right times. You will have the ability to accept all situations and self-correct accordingly.

You will enjoy the freedom and happiness to be the best you can be at what you do.

 18. STOP: LOOK: LISTEN

What are your thoughts regarding our deepest fears of not being good enough and being rejected by others?

Do you agree or disagree with them?

What are your immediate thoughts about developing your own ABC Plan?

16

Leadership withoutEGO® Model – ABC Plan in Action

• • •

To begin working on detoxing your ego, you need to start the process of understanding how your ego works, and how you can transform it. The Leadership withoutEGO® Model is your framework for change.

I'm going to illustrate this with a simple example, so that you can then apply the stages of the model to your own circumstances. Within each part (inner ego, outer ego, and transformational ego), there are a number of statements that have been highlighted to show how the model works. In the pages that follow, we'll explore each stage in detail, but this example is simply to outline the function of the model. I am going to discuss how I took Jane, prior to her final interview for promotion that she was encouraged to pursue, through the following three-part process.

Part One: Inner Ego

Jane will need to consider her two deepest fears; that is, what her inner ego is telling her. What is her greatest fear about the interview; is it not being good enough, or is it feeling rejection by employer?

Jane now stands on the first step of the model. She will need to listen to her expectations. Does Jane have a win-lose mind-set going into her interview: *'I'm successful and highly rated and I've been encouraged to go for promotion. If I don't get this promotion, I will feel deeply humiliated and judged by others.'* In contrast, if Jane has a mastery mind-set she has a compelling argument for why she should be selected for promotion while also understanding that if she is unsuccessful there will be other opportunities to build her career.

She is now within the interview process and makes a mistake. This means she has moved onto Step Two; does Jane hate making the error or does she accept and smile at it? Does this provoke a strong negative emotional reaction that subsequently hijacks her performance, leading to further errors? Or does she accept the minor error as an opportunity to increase her ability to influence the selection panel?

In millisecond speed, Jane takes time to process Step Three. *'Am I closed or open to accepting my errors and the two fears they represent? Am I closed or open to not getting the promotion, or am I avoiding the stressful feeling of being assessed?'* Is she prepared to accept what others may say if she fails to secure this new position? Now Jane has dealt with her inner ego (what she tells herself, that others cannot see) she progresses to part two: dealing with her outer ego.

Part Two: Outer Ego

Jane now progresses to Step Four: effort. Jane must put effort into aligning her feelings and actions while being assessed.

Here she needs to be consistent with what she is feeling and how she behaves. Is Jane battling with a separation between how she feels (struggling to hide her anxiety) versus what she is showing the panel? Or does she consistently show harmony between what she feels (accepting her anxiousness in the selection process) and her actions?

Jane now moves onto Step Five: fun. How much fun is Jane having during this selection interview? Does she appear miserable, tense and even sad through the interview, or does she appear to be enjoying the experience of doing something important? Once she has given her outer ego consideration, she must now focus on how she can influence and inspire the panel to select her.

Part Three: Transformational Ego

Jane must consider Step Six: give. How can she use all her experience to enthuse the panel about what she can do in the new role for the benefit of others? This naturally leads onto Step Seven: purpose. Jane immediately sees that the panel are enjoying her presentation and she begins to feel she has a true purpose for getting the promotion.

Summit

Jane has reached altitude, appreciating the enormity of the selection process that she has just endured. She has been successful. She has learnt to operate for a purpose bigger than herself – leadership without ego. She has had a high degree of freedom by following the Seven Steps. They have enabled her to cultivate her awareness and belief and make corrections (the ABC Plan) to her inner and outer ego in order to become transformational during this selection interview experience.

 19. STOP: LOOK: LISTEN

What did you think of this example?

How easy is it to put yourself in Jane's shoes?

How difficult is it to self-correct the negative feelings and emotions that are triggered when you pursue winning?

PART FIVE

Inner Ego Programme
(What You Tell Yourself – Hidden to Others)

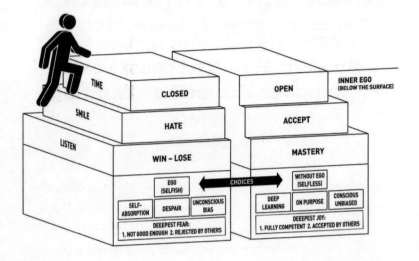

Leadership withoutEGO® Model

17

STEP ONE: Do You Listen to Whether You Are Focussed on Winning for Yourself or Winning for Others?

• • •

The first step to detox your ego is to answer the above question. If your answer is yes, you will need to honestly ask if you are winning for yourself or a team or community. If you want to win for yourself then you are operating with ego in your life; this is dangerous and must change. If, however, you are genuinely winning for a team or community, you will be free of your ego and happier in life.

'Listen' is the first characteristic of ego and it will show you how winning or losing negatively impacts our emotional world. You will see how 'win or lose' expectations are a selfish act in life. Understanding what you tell yourself when it comes to winning and losing (win-lose thinking) is key to understanding your ego response. This is the first step to seeing who you really are and how you can truly benefit from winning for others. You will see how not listening to what you tell yourself is an ego response. You need to develop a softness towards your win or lose attitude to life so that you can understand it and self-correct. Building resilience in your life by being softer towards your need to win is a difficult and time-consuming process.

Your journey starts with a coin flip and a choice.

listen

Listen Choice

Whether you know it or not, when you flip your coin of *listen* you have a choice to make. You choose either a 'win-lose' or 'mastery' mind-set. Whichever side your coin lands on will trigger a self-fulfilling prophecy. That is, you will either focus on win-lose or mastery thinking in your life.

If you choose 'I'm a winner' or 'I'm a loser' expectations in your life, you are picking an ego reaction. You will pay attention to fear in your life. This is characterised by the statement: *'I always want to win for myself.'* Clearly, such a reaction means you are in fact triggering ego in your life. Focusing on winning for yourself means you will limit your freedom, happiness and success.

However, if you are immersed in the mastery of your skills, you are choosing a selfless response, as you understand how the delivery of your skills supports your team or community. You will pay attention to joy in your life. This takes courage and is characterised by the statement: *'I always want to be the best I can be for the benefit of others.'*

By definition, elite athletes who cross the line and become world champions are, at this defining moment, immersed in the mastery of executing their skills. Here they are free, happy and ready for success in life.

Do you want to win for yourself or for a community? Are you willing and committed to stop, look and listen to your win-lose internal traffic as you pursue winning in your life? If you are, you will need to press the win-lose pause button in order to see how selfish or selfless you are.

A Personal Experience of Expectations

When I was selected to play at Lord's against Pakistan, then world champions, I couldn't wait to compete and prove myself. It was my second year and I was hungry to secure a regular spot in the first team having made my first class debut a year earlier. I had high expectations to win.

I was on autopilot, determined and striving to get in the first team and establish myself as a cricketer. Although I had played lots of second eleven cricket, I had only made a few first team appearances. At this stage, I still had no idea that fear was playing a major role in my performance and life; I thought I knew everything, and saw the world as either winners or losers. I had a low level of emotional awareness and was quite closed during this period. I refused to be a loser, so I was determined to work harder at my game to ensure I had success. I would work and work and work to improve. I would allow nothing to stand in the way. All I really wanted to do was win and play at my best for the county I had supported as a boy at Lord's, the home of cricket.

I had an air of nervous anticipation about what the day

would bring. I believed a winning performance was needed. This only added to my self-imposed pressure. I was opening the bowling and was very anxious and tense. A large crowd was making themselves heard as I tried to bowl wicket-taking deliveries against these world champion cricketers. Here was my chance and I didn't want to blow it. However, the harder I tried, the worse it got, as the players took to my bowling like ducks to water. 'Here we go again,' I thought. Something was missing but I didn't know what. Just as with my first class debut, I had no rhythm, I wasn't relaxed, and I was really stressed – not free to express myself.

It also became obvious to me that some of my teammates were appearing a bit disgruntled with me as I tried to bowl as fast as possible but failed to be effective. On reflection, I have come to understand that a mere sideways glance from someone in my team started the process of self-doubt. The inevitable statements began: 'I'm not good enough to be here', 'they look like they're not rating me'. There was an air of disappointment mixed with frustration at my work, especially from the captain. I felt like I was choking. This was not going according to plan. I felt alone and isolated and was feeling very low in myself. I tried to get angry with myself in an attempt to pep myself up. 'Why is this happening to me again? Come on,' I said to myself. All I wanted to do was to take wickets, stay in the first team, build my career in the game and secure a long-term contract. I felt like I deserved to be there but I was battling with the game, my opponents and myself. I was at war not only with myself but everyone else. 'Come on, come on,' I repeated angrily to myself, trying to force myself to do better. I needed and wanted to prove I could play. I started to question myself even more; am I just not good enough at this level, I asked, as my deliveries disappeared to the boundary. Why is my passion turning into a living nightmare? I didn't look to anyone else while my performance was stuttering. I put a brave face on it and simply told myself it just wasn't my day. I was very defensive and down.

So whilst I was overjoyed at running out on the hallowed turf playing against an international team I'd seen so many times as a boy on the television, I was equally disappointed and frustrated that I wasn't free to express myself to my full potential. I was so focused on winning and becoming the best fast bowler I could be. Every time I bowled, I tried to be faster and more accurate than the time before; getting wickets for my county was my goal and winning was everything to me. Unfortunately, I didn't take a wicket and the game faded out to a draw. I felt gutted that the results didn't match my expectations.

I have come to see the dangers of a 'win-lose' attitude in life. I grew up valuing winning – losing was not acceptable in my home growing up. Everything I did was characterised by my drive, focus and determination in order to achieve things. I wanted to create the positive reaction in others. Unfortunately, it wasn't enough as losing created more negative and hostile judgements of me. Here I had achieved my dream of playing cricket at Lord's against some of my cricketing heroes and I still felt the negative judgements from others. I had worked extremely hard to be the best but it simply wasn't good enough – there was something missing. At the time, I had no understanding of the 'something missing' element of my game.

20. STOP: LOOK: LISTEN

Can you relate to this?

Have you made similar assumptions of working hard but not getting what you want from life?

Can you think of a time when your greatest dream became your greatest fear?

I was both frustrated and annoyed at not being able to find that elusive 'missing something' to my game. After a dozen or so overs I was taken out of the attack, triggering a fresh round of self-criticism as I walked with my head down towards the boundary fence. How funny life is; at the same time as presenting me with my greatest dream, it presented me with my greatest fear – what a contradiction. I took this experience into my work now as a psychologist working with current cricketers.

Many years later, I got the privilege of working with a player returning to international Test cricket. I got a chance to compare how he was dealing with a return to international cricket with my attempt at playing first class cricket. Although these were at different levels, we both experienced the same contradiction. That is, how do you cope when your greatest dream becomes your greatest fear? We both shared and discussed this. The player had a win-lose expectation regarding his return to international cricket. He had made his international debut over ten years before, and now he was returning for his next game – unbelievable.

During this period he had put all his energies into first

class cricket and been very successful with a fantastic record, playing freely and winning many matches for the teams he played for. He had built a fantastic career through hard work, tenacity and skill. However, he had major trepidation and concern about his return to the top of his sport. We discussed switching attention from the win-lose to completely planning his return by focusing on the mastery of the situation. This first involved him acknowledging and celebrating his win-lose attitude during his previous stint in the team. We explored his interaction with other players, officials and the governing body as well as the enormity of the upcoming Test series and all the attention that came with it. He accepted that it was a great opportunity to do something different. He knew he could change his approach by shifting his expectations. This was like changing lanes on the motorway. He went from driving at 90mph in the fast lane to driving at 50mph in the slow lane.

Here he could stop, look and listen to his win-lose expectation by being able to review his win-lose attitude. He could see a compelling reason to shift his attitude towards mastery of expectations. This involved paying attention to the simple joy of being able to re-establish his dream of playing Test cricket. Talking this through was enlightening and gave him a sense of freedom, reducing his fears compared to when he first played Test cricket.

He began to accept how he could use this re-birth on the biggest international stage to contribute more to his team and country. We discussed how he could support the younger, more inexperienced cricketers as well as being of assistance to the coach. His role was much more than simply playing, as his off-field leadership became just as important as on-field.

It was lovely to see him gain such insight and I could see the impact this was having on how he chose to think. He was at ease, safe in the knowledge that he needed to focus on his bigger contribution to his country rather than the self-obsession of wanting success just for himself. This was a breakthrough in his thinking. We continued to have little chats over the course of the Test series covering potential issues and finding a way to increase his awareness, belief and correction over his ego. In the end, he accepted that while there were no easy solutions to his situation, and he didn't necessarily feel better, he had changed his win-lose attitude about his re-entry into Test cricket and he achieved success.

Today, I have come to understand that I can help by generating a deep level of self-awareness that a focus on winning for oneself is a problem. I had a win-lose way of thinking in the past and it created stress and discomfort. As a practising psychologist now, I see that others think in a similar way to how I used to. My mission is to help others appreciate that a deep level of self-correction to a mastery of skills and relationships is required.

You will need to get completely immersed in the joy of mastery of your gifts for the benefit of others. Choosing an inner freedom to simply become the best you can be leads to greater levels of happiness and purpose in your life regardless of what you do. It is an invitation to take a journey of personal transformation from a selfish to a selfless perspective.

Expectations in Business

I have supported leaders in business to understand the importance of changing their expectations from winning profit as an individual to winning profit as a team. Corporate life is by its very nature a selfish act of exchanging your services in return for pay. Here the win-lose mind-set is the automatic choice for most leaders and executives – especially true of sales executives who are employed to use their expertise to increase new sales for their business. Competition is fierce, with each sales person wanting to increase his or her sales at all costs. Many organisations thrive on the win-lose culture, each sales person selfishly pushing for deals. In these win-at-all-costs cultures, winners are celebrated when they achieve their sales quotas every month, quarter and year. They are competitive environments where only the strong survive. In contrast, losers are seen as weak and inferior due to their poor sales. And in most cases, their results are not acceptable to the business. These environments induce high levels of stress and discomfort. Either trying to fight for business and succeed or trying to get a stay of execution due to poor performance.

Long-Term Business Mission

I see lots of conflict as a result of different expectations between sales and other departments across many organisations. I have spent many hours, for example, trying to support sales staff in conflict situations with either technical or operational departments of their organisation. Once again the strong win-lose nature of sales puts sales people on a head-on collision with others. Under these conditions, sales people can become very selfish as they fight to achieve their target. In contrast, technical/finance departments have a very different emphasis. They try to slow everything down, much to the annoyance of the sales staff.

21. STOP: LOOK: LISTEN

What type of organisation do you represent?

Is your work culture focused on the sales, operations or technical aspect of work?

What is the critical history of your organisation? How is it reflected in your day to day working?

When you talk through the need to sustain profit for generations to come you get a very different reaction. One global client I work with has the following mantra: 'We are not here for thirty years, we are going to be here for over a hundred years.' This organisation has a focus to serve its community worldwide to leave a legacy for generations to follow. It is not just about making profit for the sake of profit. It is about what this profit represents in sustaining the lives of many workers around the world. This is much more towards being selfless in the pursuit of organisational mastery from both a product and people point of view. Clearly, attrition rates are low and staff love being a part of something much bigger.

It has been very rewarding to see executives shift their emotional world from a win-lose to a mastery perspective. One senior executive I worked with relaxed and shifted his thinking away from 'it's all about me winning my next position' to 'it's all about mastery of the business and people'. He set about making big changes to how he delivered in his role, being less concerned with his own need for recognition through promotion. Over many years of service he was invited to sit at the top table by being appointed MD of the UK subsidiary. He was more open to seeing how his emotional pain was affecting his need to win by securing the necessary promotion. However, once he released the block on his emotions he understood the choice of how to master building his organisation over the long term. This changed his thinking and ultimately led to him getting the promotion he aspired to. Today, he is enjoying being totally aligned to the organisational mandate and so the UK organisation is making a great contribution to the long-term legacy of its global brand.

This individual, as well as many others, have all come to the realisation that being self-absorbed and selfish not only led to unhappiness but also to poor business results. When they are able to align both their personal and professional mastery they became free and much happier. Their joy was like a magnet as they continued to inspire others to achieve more. They understood that serving others felt great. As a result, they paid great attention to working more selflessly. This created a self-fulfilling prophecy as their staff also grew as human beings. High performance was the natural by-product of this long-term approach.

This example clearly illustrates that helping leaders shift their way of working to a more caring transformational style, that embraces mastery, drives not only happiness but also performance in the workplace. Their staff feel inspired, supported, wanted and cared for. Such leadership care builds and sustains the health of any organisation.

The next section highlights how win-lose expectations can impact the quality of sibling relationships.

Expectations in Sibling Rivalry

As the middle sibling of three, I grew up in a strong sport-ing family between my brothers, mother and father. There is just a year's gap between my older brother and me, while a fifteen-year gap exists between my youngest brother and me. Before my younger brother arrived, the two of us boys grew up playing all kinds of sports together. We watched, for exam-ple, teams perform in football and cricket during World Cups and other major championships that always kept us on the edge of our seats. We would all pick a team and then the bat-tle would commence as discussion began over which team would win. We would love to watch the great West Indies cricket teams and then go out into our garden and mimic our heroes. We would compete hard and copy what we saw – the spirit was high. At the end of it we had both fought hard to win to get the bragging rights. This would extend into the eve-nings where we'd often turn our attentions to playing snooker.

We would play long into the night on the small snooker table I got for Christmas one year. These were great times, as we would try to mimic our snooker heroes, following long late nights watching who would be crowned world champion at the Crucible – the home of the World Snooker Championship. Again our competitive nature came to the fore and I loved nothing better than beating my father and brother. Equally, they loved nothing better than beating me. The laughter and banter would be great but also very hard if you were on the receiving end. Neither of us wanted to lose. No inch was given or taken.

We were aggressive and the rivalry between my older brother and me was clear to see. We both wanted to beat each other and get the upper hand regardless of what we were doing. We were close and shared many great times together. Reflecting back I now believe that wanting to beat your sibling at whatever it may be can be fraught with danger as it triggers a win-lose mind-set. Whether we know it or not, we put ourselves on a collision course with our sibling for later in life. We want to prove a point – compete. Instead, we should shift or now teach our own children to shift their thinking to a mastery mind-set. Here it is as if we are on a beach holiday, enjoying our experiences with our siblings. We need to teach them to get absorbed in whatever they're doing just for the fun of it and to be the best they can be.

 22. STOP: LOOK: LISTEN

Can you remember a time where you tried to prove yourself against your sibling?

Do you still compete with your sibling?

What is your relationship like with your sibling today?

Consequently, sibling rivalry is normal but it is unhealthy for us. Here our win-lose thinking results in us saying: 'I want to do better than my brother or sister.' Sport is littered with examples of great rivalries, sportsmen and women who compete to beat each other. However, we are beginning to see a greater level of appreciation of how siblings can put their rivalry to one side in order to work together in preparation for a major championship. Their shared experience is used to enhance how they can represent their family on the international stage. Siblings are starting to understand the power of collective excellence as a way to develop their mastery of their sport.

Here strong parents work to lower the win-lose expectations between their siblings so that their rivalry is reduced. Instead, siblings are encouraged to share more and develop a greater togetherness in order to sustain world-class performance. They develop a way of being able to cope with losing together. These families have understood the importance of being collaborative and supportive, helping both siblings perform well. By sharing the pressures of top-level sport these siblings are better positioned to choose mastery of their discipline over just the need to win. The ability to generate new learning and gain greater personal meaning allows siblings to find a new way to improve the delivery of their skills. They cultivate an intensity and much deeper commitment to the task as their sibling rivalry is replaced by an understanding of what they can do for their family, team or country. It is as if the 'family comes first' mantra facilitates a greater degree of freedom as anxiety and stress is reduced through sharing. This is in contrast to families where the sibling rivalry runs wild and interferes with freedom, happiness and success.

23. STOP: LOOK: LISTEN

What lessons can you learn about your relationship with your sibling from using this collaborative approach?

What can you do to pay greater attention to sharing more with your sibling?

How does win-lose thinking impact you at work, rest or play?

Below is an outline example of an ABC Plan for a world snooker champion. It will highlight how the individual was able to make a significant change in aligning his thinking and action to achieve more. This individual became aware of how expectations impacted his pursuit of winning in his life at the moment of crossing the line in a world championship final. Such an example will highlight our self-interest as we begin to create a harmful strong internal expectation to win.

My ABC Plan Example:
A Snooker World Champion

I was delighted to help a world number seven snooker player, in preparation for the upcoming World Snooker Championships. I would visit him at his club and watch him practise. We would discuss all things regarding his preparation. When he started his world championship campaign we would begin by speaking over the phone following one of his matches where I would watch him on TV and give feedback regarding his performance. We would go into detail. For example, we had one exchange about the number of times he would feather a ball (moving your cue up and down towards the white ball until you strike it). His coach had the view that this should be consistent, citing examples of world-class players who feathered a consistent number of times in all situations. We would have a healthy discussion about what was the ideal number of times he feathered. I collected data first by watching his early matches on the TV and then in the later rounds I would sit in the guest balcony at tournaments and collect his feathering data. We would then have a thorough discussion about it. What prevailed was clear evidence that the number of times he feathered was not an issue; instead what was key was the importance of the shot. So when the shot had most meaning he would feather for the longest period of time until he felt ready to strike the white ball. It was intriguing to see that when it was a critical shot he consistently feathered longer in order to make sure the shot was the best it could be. This gave him clarity about the discussion over feathering as he continued his progress to the final of the World Championships.

The final, an event I'd watched so many times on the TV, was at 6.00pm. I was in my hotel room just opposite the Crucible, the home of the snooker World Championships. I was fortunate to be working with the world number seven player; I felt hugely privileged and was enjoying the seventeen-day journey with the player into the final. I became aware that I felt very calm and relaxed about what was to come. It was as if I had seen it happening. He was ready; he was at his peak, he knew his game and he was physically fit. He had completed hours and hours of training through swimming and yoga.

He had a great team and I was glad to be a part of it. It felt like something special was about to happen.

Inside the Crucible you could cut the atmosphere with a knife. I went to the guest balcony in readiness for his entrance into the arena. The stage was set, a thousand or so people crammed into such a small and intimidating place. The music blared out for his entrance and then a hush descended upon the Crucible as the final match began.

1: Awareness

The final is the best of thirty-five frames and the match ebbed and flowed. The aim was to win eighteen frames in order to be crowned world champion. The tension was rising. At 15-15, the world number seven player made a hundred break to go 16-15 up. It was difficult to pick a winner. His opponent, the world number five player, won the next frame for it go 16-16, only for number seven to make a large break to go 17-16 up. At this stage, I had moved from the balcony to the changing room, watching this close match unfold on a small monitor alongside his manager and coach.

The number five got in early but missed a red ball into the back ball pocket. The number seven got another opportunity, only needing one more frame, and you could see that he was becoming anxious that the finishing line was fast approaching. Number seven was precise and deliberate; although there was lots of tension and pressure, he was slowly growing his lead as his opponent waited for him to make a mistake. His opponent looked down and dejected. We all jumped up when number seven missed, though, and number five was back; he potted a red and a black and got perfect position on the next red. However, he then suddenly missed – the pressure of the situation affecting one of the greatest players to ever play the game.

The number seven came back to the table, needing only a few more balls to become world champion. His opponent simply put his head down in frustration and disappointment and his chances of winning the world championship again looked like it had slipped away. The number seven potted a red and had a straight black off its spot. I'm sure he had seen his name on the title. '*This to become world champion,*' he said to himself. He cued the white ball and struck right across it and immediately jumped up in anguish as he watched the black ball wobble in the jaws of the pocket. He put his hand on his head and cue in the air in sheer disbelief as he walked back to his corner. As he sat in his chair you could see that he was processing the thought that he had just lost the world championship that was right there for the taking. He was down and out.

Simultaneously, the world number five player jumped up and eagerly approached the table, while back in the changing room we watched in disbelief and total shock. Our man's coach, feeling the pressure, shouted in frustration and stormed out of the changing room. His normally reserved manager began to show signs of disbelief, suggesting he didn't know what the number seven would do if he didn't win it.

The number five polished off the remaining balls to take the match into the final frame at 17-17. Number seven had had two good chances to become world champion and had come up short, while his opponent was focused and happy to get his hand on the table in this dramatic frame. The world number five sat back in his chair, clearly relieved at taking the match into a deciding frame.

The early exchanges in the final frame of the match were a tense affair with both players missing opportunities to build a sizeable lead. Each player's rhythm and freedom were affected by the importance of the final frame of this long match. It was well into the early hours and the match had been an all-time epic, the snooker stars like two heavyweight boxers slugging it out. Clearly both players were suffering major stress as they fought to cross the line first and become world champion.

2. Belief
It was obvious that number seven thought his chances of becoming a world champion were ebbing away. He was playing one of the greatest players ever and he had blown chances of winning it across the last two frames. Now into the final frame it became a lottery of who would get a chance to build a significant break. It was as if he was playing that final frame with a no-hope-of-winning attitude. He let go of self-importance. He began to accept his chances of winning were all but gone.

3. Correction
This resulted in the world number seven getting immersed in the mastery of just potting one ball at a time. He was simply pleased and relieved to be at the table and potting a ball and getting a position for the next ball so he could pot that. He no longer thought about winning. Each pot appeared to be making it harder for his opponent who was at this stage looking really downhearted.

The Defining Moment
Then all of a sudden, with only a few points needed, number seven missed a red down the rail. The world number five

player was sharply back at the table; he potted a red and pink which snookered the world number seven in behind the black ball. He looked long and hard at an escape and finally came up with a solution. His opponent tried again to get in behind the black with the white ball ending up in the pocket. The number seven cut a ball into the yellow pocket, which meant he now had an unassailable lead, so his opponent walked across to concede and congratulate him. The lights came on and number seven turned to his opponent, shaking his head in disbelief; he had just become world champion. He was shaking his head as if he had just been woken up from a dream. His daughter ran into his arms to celebrate, I was still in the changing room with his manager and we immediately rushed out onto the Crucible stage to celebrate with him. It was an amazing euphoric occasion. I felt excited, emotional and wanted to scream out with joy but when I got into the Crucible I realised the enormity of the place and came to a silent and sudden halt.

As I looked around, I could see every person's eyes. I felt slightly intimidated and it gave me an immediate feeling of what it must be like to play where everyone is on top of you. You need nerves of steel. As the acceptance speeches were delivered I felt so proud to be a part of such a great occasion, as if I was watching one of my children achieve something special for the very first time. It was great. Everyone was so happy for him and the celebrations had started in earnest. I shot back to my hotel room to change and then proceeded to the Champion's Reception.

It was fascinating later at the reception celebration to talk with the multiple world champion and current world number five player, who was clearly very disappointed and down regarding the result. I was amazed at how self-critical he was considering he had won it on numerous occasions. It was like he found it difficult to reconcile losing it, simply saying, 'I wasn't good enough; he deserved it – I was rubbish.' Wow – arguably this is one of the greatest players of all time being really critical of himself. He made a great speech, and then the new world champion followed this by doing all the necessary pleasantries and thank yous.

I was sat for the evening on his family's table, the champagne flowing, and we were all so proud. I was so happy and contented being a part of such a great occasion, that I didn't even have a drink and stayed drinking sparkling water to savour the moment. It was awesome – and surprisingly it felt better than achieving my own dream of playing first class cricket at Lord's.

As the evening came to a close, the new world champion and I sat and reflected on his experience. His victory came from a reduction in expectations regarding winning – he had suddenly 'let go', when, during the final frame, his acceptance that he might have missed his opportunity to win shifted his emotional world. He had a sense of calmness and got out of the way of his emotions. This allowed him to objectively focus on the task at hand – potting balls. Although he was unaware of it at the time, he had truly learnt to operate without ego.

Your ABC Plan:
Pressing Your Win-Lose Pause Button

You need to ask yourself the following questions: do you want to beat others? Or do you want to be the best that you can be at what you do?

If you have answered 'yes' to both of these questions you have a big problem.

From both a personal and professional perspective, I have found that striving to beat someone else causes conflict and disharmony. This is because trying to win directly competes with our desire to become the best we can be. Focusing on winning and being the best are two competing forces. Here you will be pulled in two different directions. On the one hand, you could win and not perform at your best at something; while on the other, you could lose but deliver a masterful performance at something. The question is, which is better? I know from my own experiences that winning against another person was all that mattered. I was not really bothered if my performance was poor so long as I won. Have you experienced a similar situation?

The point here is that our high expectations to beat others is a real distraction to our true purpose in life. By competing and beating others, it makes us feel good about ourselves. However, this is ego driven and our success is short-lived, inconsistent and not sustainable. This creates real stress in our lives that can potentially lead to poor mental health. We get so consumed with a desire to win it can be like a virus attacking our body – at millisecond speed, our thoughts can put us out of kilter. For example, the runner starts to think about beating teammates instead of concentrating on his or her times. The sales executive thinks about thrashing his competition and winning market share. Two siblings show the signs of strain as one attempts to exert control over the other in their relationship. In each example, the win-lose expectations undermine freedom, happiness and success. So the runner records a poorer time. The sales executive doesn't express himself freely to win the business and the siblings' relationship suffers a breakdown. What is your experience?

Instead, we need to switch our expectations to a mastery mind-set. Here we embrace the mastery of our skills and life for our long-term sustainable development. As a result, you will move away from the immediate thoughts of winning or losing at something to how it will feel if you could develop a depth of mastery about what you do in order that others may benefit.

This means that choosing mastery over the win-lose mind-set will have tremendous beneficial results. For example, the runner will pay attention to his or her breathing, running stride pattern and rhythm instead of worrying about what their competitor is doing. The sales executive concentrates on a deep understanding of their customer's needs instead of worrying about what their main rivals are doing. And finally, the siblings spend time talking through their differences and how to improve their togetherness.

 24. STOP: LOOK: LISTEN

What can you do to create more mastery in both your personal and professional life?

Why not try to make contact with someone and talk about all the times you competed against them?

Then ask them what you could do to develop a more masterful relationship.

In conclusion, by pressing the pause button we can begin to see how concentrating on beating others interferes with our pursuit of being the best. It creates stress and fear that is seriously unhealthy for us. Here our ego is triggering a *'I want to beat him or her'* attitude that is not in our best long-term interest. You must listen to your expectations and accept that a focus on winning for one's self will hinder your performance. You must begin to really see how mastery of what you do can truly benefit yourself and others and give you greater freedom, happiness and success.

ABC Plan – Win-Lose Expectations

Accepting your win-lose attitude, behaviour, values and beliefs

So, by working through your own Awareness, Belief and Correction (ABC) Plan you will be in a better position to see how your win-lose attitude impacts on your life.

Awareness (A): Win-Lose Attitude

You will need to examine your attitude towards winning and losing in life. Are you happy when you win and sad when you lose? How aware are you of seeing the world only filled with winners or losers? If you are unaware of your win-lose attitude, you will most definitely be operating with self-importance or selfishly.

Belief (B): Win-Lose Behaviour

You will need to assess your winning and losing behaviour. Do you ignore your frustrations when you win or lose? Are you able to accept losing in your life? If you ignore your win-lose behaviour, you are almost certainly functioning with self-importance or selfishly.

Correction (C): Win-Lose Values and Beliefs

You will need to consider what are your underlying values and beliefs about things you win and lose at in life. You will need to consider how you can align your attitudes, behaviours, values and beliefs in order to embrace both winning and losing. If you choose to cultivate an ABC Plan you will actively seek to understand winning and losing in a healthier way. This is an essential self-correction needed to shift your values and beliefs towards winning for the benefit of others. The aim of this process is to shift from a winning for oneself (selfish) perspective to a winning for others (selfless) perspective. This will give you a deeper level of joy and contentment.

Are you willing and committed to stop and look at winning and losing in the pursuit of winning in life?

Imagine you had a device like a TV remote control that you could use to stop, rewind or fast forward live play, like in the film *Click*. In this instance though, live play constitutes your win-lose behaviour. What happens to your behaviour when you are doing something important, like chasing a victory? Its other functionality would include: a super slow motion button so that you could review your performance before, during and after winning or losing at something. It also has a pause button so that you could view a static image of yourself doing something important. We can all pretend to use this imaginary device to carry out lots of self-observation regarding what we do.

I worked on a TV diving show where the celebrities

were able to view their dives as they immediately came out of the water. This instant video feedback was crucial to accelerate their learning of each dive. They were able to see themselves in different positions at the start and through the air, and were able to assess their entry into the water, specifically seeing if they entered in a straight line, head first. They intensely assessed their diving and where they should spend their time to improve. We can do exactly the same in our imagination. We need to look at our win-lose behaviour to understand our inner world and what choices we make on a day-to-day basis.

What emotion do you display when you win and lose when you are doing something important? What comes to mind? Are you happy or sad when you win or lose? Do you get angry when things don't go right?

ABC Plan Summary

Using your imaginary TV remote control try to observe your attitude to winning and losing, specifically when you are doing something important. Ask yourself the following questions:

- *What can I see about the way I win and lose in life?*
- *What do I like and dislike about my approach to winning and losing?*
- *What is my attitude and behaviour like under pressure?*
- *Do I get angry, happy or sad under the strain of needing to win?*

Step One: Press Pause

Can you find someone, or even a small group, to discuss your answers with? If so, what can you share with others about the way you win and lose in life? What do others say about your winning mentality in life?

What do you take away from pressing the pause button? Why do you approach winning and losing the way you do? How can you self-correct your attitude to winning by taking a more masterful perspective?

Regardless of whether you are playing sport or in business or education or simply at home with your family, hunting winning increases the likelihood that your automatic behaviour becomes dysfunctional. The need to win puts an extraordinary strain on how you act. Using your TV remote control you can learn to see how your behaviour affects those around you. Do you behave selfishly or do you think of others in your most pressing need to win at something? What are your thoughts on the following questions?

- Do you like or dislike viewing your behaviour while you are doing something important?
- What do you see – are you mad, sad or happy?
- Are you shocked, surprised or happy at seeing what you do under pressure?
- Are you spending the time behaving the way you want to?
- Do you have all the time in the world to do the things you want to do?

- Are you negative, positive or indifferent about your use of time?
- Is there alignment between your win-lose attitude and how you perform?
- How is your win-lose attitude consuming your thoughts?
- Where are the examples of your win-lose attitude and behaviour operating in life?
- What do the questions reveal about your win-lose expectations in life?

Listen Mindfulness

*Imagine a world where it wasn't about whether you won or lost at something. Instead, everyone's focus and energy was on whether they had mastered what they were doing. Over this **first Step**, gaining a greater mastery over what you do is your focus. Try to plot how you will improve something important in your life. Follow the line of questions:*

1. *What do you want to master and why?*
2. *Do you want to win for yourself?*
3. *Do you want to win for others?*
4. *What normally happens when you get it wrong?*
5. *Do you feel incompetent when doing it?*
6. *Do you feel judged by others when doing it?*
7. *What do you contribute to society as a result of your mastery?*

So, which way does your coin end up? Do you focus on winning for yourself? Or do you want to perform at your best in life for others? Of course we all like to think we can win and be the best all at the same time. However, I have discovered that winning and becoming the best are separate things. I have experienced many occasions where I have won and not been the best. Equally, I have lost many times but performed at my best. This creates a major conflict for us. Winning for oneself puts us into a selfish mode and leads to long-term negative health consequences. Do you have similar experiences?

Please select which statement best reflects you when you are about to do something important in life: 'I've got to win today,' or, 'I'm focused on performing at my best today.'

Choice 1. 'I've got to win today'

Win-lose mind-set: Focusing on winning triggers our ego (self interest). This brings our attention to the thought of beating others. You will enter a world of fighting for survival. Here your purpose is to win and succeed over others. You experience relief at winning. Your joy is short-lived as your immediate attention turns to the next chance of winning. In fact, winning feels like an anti-climax. Throughout the pursuit of winning you will experience high levels of stress and burnout – at times you feel totally flat. You constantly feel something is missing. Quality performances are inconsistent. You are not always happy, and at times, experience a low regard for self. You feel stuck, as if each day is a repeat of the day before – like in *Groundhog Day*. You are highly self critical and you take no time for reflection. Finally, you feel incredibly judged by others.

Choice 2. 'I'm focused on performing at my best today'

Mastery mind-set: Focusing on becoming the best you can be allows you to operate without ego. Your performance is about the joy of improving your previous best. This is like an artist working on his masterpiece daily for the pure pleasure of producing something beautiful. You are living life to the fullest, engaged and enjoying every moment of performing. You hold a greater vision and understanding about your contribution to performing and life. You know there is a greater purpose for what you do than simply winning and beating others. You gain a deeper sense of perspective and balance. You are excited by each challenge. Your performance becomes consistent and the quality remains high. You will be free to express your skills and talents and stress will have little impact on you. You will feel happier and hold a higher self-regard. You will take time for reflection and view your performance from an appreciative perspective. You will not feel impacted by the judgement of others.

Conclusion

How does it feel to observe your win-lose behaviour from a mindfulness perspective? What is your physical reaction to a difficult situation? What does it say about you? The more self-observation of our win-lose attitude we make, the greater acceptance we can gain about what we do and why we do it. The celebrities on the diving show became more relaxed about their diving when they accepted their win-lose attitude by watching themselves diving and figuring out how to master each dive in a short period of time.

Greater acceptance of our win-lose attitude and behaviour leads to greater satisfaction and autonomy, which in turn leads to greater freedom and happiness. Here the individual gets immersed in the mastery of a task for the sheer delight and pleasure of doing something incredibly well. The fear of being criticised, judged or rejected has been minimised and the person can slowly start to restore their mental wellbeing.

18

STEP TWO: Do You Smile at Your Errors?

• • •

The second step to detox your ego is to answer the above question. If you answer yes, then you are well on your way to being free of your ego and happier in life. If, however, your immediate response is no, then you are definitely choosing to function on ego. Here you are attempting to pursue winning for yourself. Hating your errors is dangerous and must change. Being open to your immediate reaction to mistakes is key to understanding your ego. This is the second step to seeing who you really are and how you can truly benefit from winning for others. 'Error' is the second characteristic of ego and it shows you how errors cause emotional pain in life. You will see how hating your errors is a selfish act in life. By reading through this step you will see how your reaction or response to errors indicates the maturity of your emotional world. You need to develop a softness towards your errors so that you can understand them and self-correct. Building resilience in your life by being softer towards your errors is a difficult and time-consuming process.

Your journey starts with a coin flip and a choice.

Smile Choice

Whether you know it or not, when you flip your coin of *smile* you have a choice to make. You choose either a 'hate errors' or 'accept errors' mind-set. Whichever side your coin lands on will trigger a self-fulfilling prophecy. That is, you will either focus on errors or what you can learn from making mistakes in your life.

. If you choose to dislike your errors in life, you are choosing an ego reaction. You are choosing to pay attention to fear in your life. This is characterised by the statement: *'I hate making mistakes.'* Clearly, such a reaction means you are in fact ignoring great learning in your life. A hatred for errors means you will limit your freedom, happiness and success.

However, if you are open to generating learning from your errors, you are choosing a selfless response as you begin to find a way to be even more helpful to your community. You are choosing to pay attention to joy in your life. This takes courage and is characterised by the statement: *'I am fully open and alert to learning from my mistakes.'*

By definition, elite athletes who cross the line and become world champions are, at this defining moment, open to accepting their errors. Here, they are free, happy and ready for success in life.

25. STOP: LOOK: LISTEN

Do you hate or accept your errors?

Are you willing and committed to exploring what your errors mean in your pursuit of winning in your life?

If you are, you will need to appreciate, even celebrate, your errors in order to generate greater learning.

A Personal Experience of Errors

I hated making mistakes in my cricket, and would regularly berate myself when things didn't go according to plan. Why didn't I do this, or that? Why do others affect me? I thought over and over about how I could improve things – I was a constant worrier. I loathed the feeling of failing at the thing I loved. As a result, I avoided the real truth about what my errors represented.

Does this ring any bells with you?

I was just entering my second year in county cricket and I was in the squad for a one-day game at the Oval cricket ground in London. I was excited and nervous all at the same time as I drove to the Oval in the misty early morning. I arrived at the ground, entering through the main gates and finding a parking bay around the left-hand side of the ground. I had achieved some previous success playing cricket at the Oval, so I was hoping that I would get the nod to open the bowling for my county in this national competition.

I made my way up to the changing rooms high up in

the main stand and onto the balcony to survey the ground. It looked splendid and I couldn't wait to get out to warm up. I eagerly got changed and made my way down to the practice nets. It was a big game between two rival clubs and the crowds were already gathering – maybe it would be an even bigger game for me. Would I be playing or not? As I prepared to bowl in the practice nets, I was thrilled to be there as I looked around the ground and took in the amazing atmosphere. I ran in and bowled as quickly as I could at our batsmen, some of whom were England internationals; I was keen to make an impression on the captain.

About thirty minutes before the start of the match the captain approached me to say I was in. I was playing! This gave me a surge of energy and excitement – as well as a shot of apprehension: 'Right, this is my chance to make a big impression.' I continued warming up with even greater intensity. When I bowled a poor ball I immediately got very self-critical. I would try even harder to get it right. I didn't want to make any mistakes. Thirty minutes later, we'd won the toss and were fielding. I took the field and immediately felt the electric atmosphere. I was opening the bowling. The wicket was towards the far right-hand side of the Oval square. I thought the boundary fence was rather close but continued to mark my run up out and get ready for my first ball. Errors in my game occurred immediately as the quality players in the opposition took to my deliveries like ducks to water. I was hit for consistent runs and as I tried to admonish myself for my errors, they simply kept on coming. I could see and feel the frustration of my teammates who felt that we were immediately losing momentum in the game with such a poor start. As a result, the captain withdrew me from bowling after only four overs.

I was devastated. I felt terrible. Not only had I let myself down but I had let my teammates down. I was angry with myself. As the game progressed, I was full of self-criticism and frustration regarding how I had performed. I constantly tried to get the attention of the captain to bring me back on to bowl. I wanted to rectify my awful situation. Eventually the captain called me back to bowl towards the end of the innings. At this stage, two England internationals were at the crease and I was determined to put things right. I ran in extra hard, thinking that I would bowl shorter deliveries than in my opening spell. However, these deliveries were pounced upon and each batsman took great delight in pumping me to all parts of the ground. My desire to put things right didn't work. Instead it led to a greater level of errors, either bowling too full or too short. This was difficult to accept and I totally unravelled mentally.

I walked off the pitch feeling pretty low and frustrated, having only bowled six overs out of a maximum of eleven. The opposition had got a very big score and we were being asked serious questions about how we would respond. My level of self-criticism was incredibly high; I sat in the changing room at the end of the game that we clearly lost, when everyone else had left pretty quickly, and contemplated what had just happened. Not only had I bowled poorly but I also got caught out for nought. The game couldn't have been worse for errors, everything that could go wrong had done. I was very unhappy and down with my performance. As I walked across the ground back to my car, I considered how I could learn from such a nightmare experience. I couldn't find any positives. I got in my car and drove home.

Over the next two-year period my performances fluctuated – one game I'd be taking wickets and doing well, the next game finding no rhythm or timing and performing poorly. At the end of my second year, management called me into a meeting to inform me that my contract would not be renewed. I was devastated, as I had only experienced a handful of first team games, yet I was the leading wicket taker in the second team. They suggested that the reason for not renewing my contract was based solely on my first team appearances.

This was a very low point in my career. I did indeed feel a failure and I totally blamed myself. The chairman asked me what I was going to do; I replied I needed to continue to pursue my cricket in order to understand what my errors were. I couldn't let it go. I needed to know that I had tried everything to rectify my mistakes and make a success of my cricketing career. I needed to get away from the feeling of being labelled a failure. In fact, I needed to get away from being labelled anything at all. It reminded me of experiences growing up with teachers who regularly negatively judged who I was and what I could do.

I wrote to all counties looking for an opportunity; at six county cricket clubs, the coaches gave me advice on my technique and what I needed to do to improve and restart my career. It was not until I visited and bowled at a county in the Midlands, where a former England international bowler was the cricket manager, that I got a new opportunity. He suggested that I had something to offer the club and that he could help me achieve my cricketing ambition.

I was overjoyed at hearing such news. The feeling of my past failures slowly ebbed away as this new county offered me a contract. I moved up to the county to pursue my ambition of playing first class cricket. I felt renewed and glad to have another chance to prove myself. On top of this the cricket manager had got feedback from my coach at my previous county saying that I could bowl and the club might have actually let me go prematurely. This was indeed great feedback. I also got some great feedback from a star player that I played club cricket with. He advised me about what I needed to do to make a better fist of it second time round. Whilst some of this was painful, it was an important indicator of how I managed to stay out of the way of myself. I would later take my experience with errors into my psychology role.

Here is one example of my work where I returned to cricket as the team psychologist for the county I played for over fifteen years earlier. It was a hot summer morning and I had been invited to conduct a session with a squad of county cricketers, involving several international England cricketers, both senior players and rising England stars. The session focused on the question: what does collective excellence in the team look like? This initially created a quiet and intense session where the questions regarding things they felt about each other were unravelled. In addition, areas that put the team in conflict were also unpacked, such as the impact of England stars returning from international duty. Such issues stimulated lots of debate where individuals could express their frustrations in a safe and respectful way.

Both players who had captained their country took the lead in the discussions. The other senior England players then chipped in with their views. As the discussion evolved, some hidden issues began to surface and we were able to get some real views expressed about some of the problems the team were facing. Everyone was encouraged to voice their opinion. This was a liberating experience where the elephant in the room became clear for everyone to see and was addressed.

Players and staff left the meeting feeling buoyed by the experience as issues that were previously buried, over long time frames, came to the surface. This created much-needed conversation and togetherness that led to more intense banter. It was good to see everyone feeling much more engaged with one another. The team was indeed happier being more open and sharing issues that had previously been avoided.

I was astonished that even world-class players were making the same errors as I had done all those years back. It appeared that the only difference was they were operating at a much higher level. I felt like I was on a mission to ensure the team increasingly became aware of the dangers of these mistakes that put the individual ahead of the team without anyone really noticing it. I was excited by the proposition that I could help others learn from my own experiences of errors in cricket. I found that my level of self-importance was also prevalent with others across many different environments.

 26. STOP: LOOK: LISTEN

What similar or different experiences have you had?

How does it feel to underachieve at something you love?

What have you learnt about yourself through your underachievement in life?

Errors in Business

Helping executives to appreciate errors in business is a difficult process. Many executives don't admit to making mistakes
and look to deflect attention to others. This is an indication
of emotional pain and blockages in thinking. Self-criticism
is a way of protecting oneself from and against a build up
of emotional turmoil following an error. At the Leadership
withoutEGO® retreats, I help executives unravel their below-
the-surface reactions and help them to see what their errors
represent in emotional terms. During this day away, any
immediate reaction to their errors is captured and recorded
to understand where the executive is anchored. I ask them
to explore their decision making in the lead up to the errors
and the context in which they are operating. This can result
in defensiveness and fear. Some executives are completely
closed while others are happy to take the journey of courage
and explore what can be learnt from the errors in the specific
situation. It is always interesting to see if executives are able
to review where things have not worked and what their errors
really show.

I always find, at the end of the retreat, they are better able
to take the brave decision to embrace what their errors really
represent. This is usually very difficult and uncomfortable.
However, in facilitating constructive debate, an executive is
able to really see how to improve processes, structures or performance. It does take courage and high self-regard to consider errors in the workplace, as most people are very fearful
about being judged by others. It always leads to discussion
about being accountable and responsible to others for the
decisions made within their organisation. Executives who

show an appreciation of errors have a strong desire to generate as much learning as possible following an error. They create organisational freedom by really embracing what errors indicate, and are resilient to the judgement of others by being open, accountable and responsible for them. Helping executives understand their errors is always tough but inspiring, as this example shows.

Helping a partner in a property company better understand his errors was a hard but rewarding experience. He had a very clear view of what was required to perform well as an architect through his years of training. He was bright and very successful. He was meticulous about the detail and demanded much from his staff. He was uncompromising in his approach to winning new business and delivering project drawings on time, on cost and with absolute perfection. He set incredibly high standards and he didn't suffer fools gladly. At times this got him into all sorts of bother. His passion for quality standards would spill over into open confrontation with other members of staff and other partners. His main agitators were two partners – one architect and one engineer. The examples of conflict included an absolute intolerance of their errors. So if they had produced something with a slight design fault he would be really upset. If they didn't deliver the project on time it would trigger an enraged bust up. If they didn't get the pricing of projects right this would also lead to a heated exchange. In fact, anything that he felt was wrong he would instantly turn to anger and vent his frustration at the error of their ways. Consequently, staff would be very nervous and anxious of any interaction with him. They would ensure they did their best to get it right. Everyone knew he hated errors, however small they may be.

As a result, the CEO decided that help for him was required. I met with him initially to scope out what his thoughts were. I also met the chief protagonists and the CEO to get a richer, fuller picture of what was happening. Through all these discussions a very clear picture was emerging. A leadership development programme was tailored and this partner was invited along. This included observations of his work patterns and meetings as well as individual sessions to better understand his style of interaction and why errors had such an adverse effect on him.

By focusing on what his errors with his peers were, he was able to reveal something about his emotional pain in life. His intolerance of others and their mistakes was an indication of something much deeper in his life. He was prepared to explore this and take the time to understand what he was blind to and why he chose anger and frustration. Through the process he began to see and accept that the incredibly high standards set for him both at home as a child and through his early work experiences had contributed to his intolerant attitude later in his life. He was given insight about world champions being flexible and open to their errors as a way of creating a new way of learning.

This initially created further discussion and a non-accepting attitude. He had believed that the best in the world just got things right. The quality standard was set incredibly high. While this was true, I explained that it was their ability to be open and accept when things went wrong and then to generate the learning to self-correct the situation. I asked him how we would see this in his work and relationships with colleagues? Consequently, we spent lots of time drilling into the detail of his anger toward errors. This revealed some truths about his high level of self-criticism and led to discussion about being judged by others, especially in his early years growing up. What became clear was that he had inadvertently learned a rule about getting the support from others. Clearly it was not to accept any errors, as he started to explain the intolerance of errors by others. He had a deep-seated fear of not being good enough. This made him more attacking as he perpetuated the fear of significant others in his life. Such realisation helped him understand and believe that a self-correction was necessary. His hatred for errors was only generating more errors as those around him were fearful of announcing any problems. Invariably when they did they were humiliated for it. This only perpetuated his error problem.

The self-correction only occurred when he faced others and they explained all his good elements, his reaction to errors built up absolute fear in them. Hearing people say how they felt had an immediate effect. Even his PAs suggested how bad his confrontations made them feel and created a tension in the office. As a result, he became much more flexible and freer to understand the inappropriateness of his reaction to errors. He was much better at self-correcting his way of working and communicating with his peers. He generated new learning on how to communicate his concerns to his partners without them being lost in translation because of his reaction to errors. He developed a pre-warning system so that he could soft land concerning issues before he hit the rage button. Other partners were happier and the business could finally make progress on how it was delivering its overall performance. Over this period, his leadership improved as he moved away from a transactional to transformational style. Here his command and control style was replaced with the following:

- Greater understanding and empathy regarding what errors meant for him.
- Scanning staff and partners in order to become acutely aware and be sensitive to not using anger when frustrations occurred.
- Spending more time with the other architect and engineer trying to understand their context and the decisions they made.
- Extra responsibility to produce a manual on how the organisation should operate so that there was a standardised methodology across the business.

In conclusion, this partner cultivated his interest in others by understanding his own assumptions about what errors mean in his life. By deeply exploring errors he was better able to identify why he reacted the way he did. More importantly, it gave him greater empathy with others. He began to develop greater emotional currency to match his undoubted skills as an architect. He truly started to appreciate that errors are an indication that something positive needs to happen in people terms. He was able to make a big difference in the way he operated.

Elite Athlete in Error

I have had the privilege of consulting with GB divers ahead of an Olympic Games. I was asked to help them on their Olympic journey. It was fascinating to watch them at training or competing both at home competitions and European Championships and eventually at the Olympic Games. It was even more fascinating to examine their stress and specifically what they told themselves in these pressurised environments. I would work with both the divers and the coach, helping them all see the uncomfortable truth about their relationship and the high performance environment. Initially there was a lot of blaming each other regarding the divers' performance errors.

On the one hand, the coach felt annoyed that he had to be overly sensitive to his divers regarding feedback on errors and corrections they needed on their dives. He had to learn how to deliver coaching instruction that wouldn't negatively impact on the diver. In contrast, one particular diver felt angry towards what she perceived as a highly critical coach.

Anything with a hint of criticism would subsequently derail her, bringing the training session to an abrupt end. On top of this, the pressure of getting selected for the Olympic Games only intensified this problem. I was tasked with helping them to get a greater understanding of what was going on. I conducted both individual and group sessions exploring the truth of their situation. In facilitating such sessions I was able to unravel some of the hidden assumptions about their working pattern. Both the diver and the coach were in denial that they were avoiding the real issues. First, the diver's stress was heightened by the selection process for the Olympics, which meant her view was to proactively seek out any sign that would tell her she was not making the Olympic standard. If one of her dives went poorly it could potentially end the session, as she was unwilling to experience such discomfort. This meant that if she perceived the coach to be giving negative feedback she would immediately derail. This would come in the form of outbursts of rage, tears and anxiety about her future.

The solution was to draw her into seeing the emotional pain that was being hidden by her outbursts. This was a difficult first step as she took some time to accept that her outbursts were saying something else about her. She needed an alternative way of looking at herself and her problem. Through our discussion it became clear that all her life she felt incredibly judged by others. Her coach had started to judge her in the same way. She felt empty. Over a number of sessions we explored what it was like to accept and embrace this judgement. Lots of past experiences of being judged came out and she was able to see that she was making an error regarding perceived judgement. This was a great starting point.

Over the next two years she was able to see that her initial response was a self-absorbed and selfish reaction based on fear. Although she tried to appreciate that the error was a trigger for self-criticism, she still found it difficult to change. She was in an Olympic year now and the pressure still made her limit her self-care. This was discussed and alignment between her and the coach was reached on how to stop training sessions from derailing. After several years of preparation she made the GB Olympic team and went off to the games. She did herself and GB proud and although she didn't medal she had a good result. It was wonderful to watch her perform and self-correct her feelings about errors. She had achieved a satisfactory result in front of a packed stadium of 20,000 people.

My ABC Plan Example:
A GB Orienteering World Champion

Here is an outline example of ABC Plans for British Orienteering, including a GB World Orienteering Champion. It will highlight how the sport made significant changes in aligning its thinking and action from both an individual and team perspective. From an organisational level, the performance director wanted to make a smooth transition for the appointment of a new head coach to take over from a successful performance coach from Sweden. From a group level, he wanted to improve the team's togetherness. From an individual level, he wanted our best athletes to continue to improve upon their success at world level. My aim was to help the newly appointed head coach embrace a new way of working, support the team to work more effectively and help athletes to achieve more.

My work began when I was invited to deliver a workshop in Sheffield to the Great Britain orienteering team on stress management. I felt very privileged to be working with this group of elite athletes, as I was fascinated by the fact that these individuals had chosen to commit to a sport at world-class level – even though it was not classed as a professional sport. I had come from a world of working with professional footballers, cricketers, golfers and snooker players; these incredible elite athletes did their sport for pure love. They were professional in terms of the hours and hours of dedication but they were not in the sport for money and fame. They loved what they were doing, being outdoors, up a mountain, in a forest, running for hours, with just a compass and a map. It was a fascinating sport that required complete commitment.

I was truly amazed to witness their values for doing the basic things very well. They ate well, trained even better and did their rehab brilliantly – I've never seen rehab performed so meticulously as I have at Great Britain orienteering camps. They were exceptionally fit, and were able to train around their day jobs in order to become the best in the world. With the advancement of lottery funding, some of these athletes were becoming full time, although their wages didn't compare to other professional athletes.

I ran through my presentation and discussed the impact of stress on their orienteering. We created much debate and discussion about how stress can be managed better for higher, more consistent performances. I was struck by their commitment to excellence both as individuals and as a team; it was a throw-back to the time when athletes dreamt of competing without the commercialism of modern-day sport. The comparison to professional athletes was stark; no fast cars, Rolex watches or fancy jewellery – these athletes were hungry for success for the pure desire of being the best at their sport.

I loved their values and beliefs. This first session led to more interaction and before I knew it I was hooked on orienteering. I travelled across the world over a seven-year period with the GB team in all their major championships, including European and World Championships. It was great fun. I would turn up at an airport somewhere in the world with my map and coordinates, and told to get to the camp, which was usually in some remote part of a country.

It was a far cry from my experiences in football and cricket, where everything was done for you and you were paid for doing it. This was a very different culture, it felt not like work but fun. The pressure was all about producing on the world level for personal pride, recognition and serving your country. I felt a little exposed and, like all elite teams, I had to learn fast. It was a great challenge and the banter was fantastic. I found myself in the heartbeat of a group of people that loved being in the outdoors in the most beautiful forests and mountains in all parts of the world. They were open, honest and hard working, completing many hours of training across weeks, months and years. We would have many discussions about sports and what constitutes fitness. It was clear to me that these were some of the fittest athletes I had ever had the pleasure of working with. They were also very bright, with most having good first or higher degrees. They were eager to grasp my ideas and thoroughly enjoyed testing whether I was any good. Coming from a ruthless sports and business background, where success was defined by how much you earned, it was a humbling and very rewarding experience that I will cherish forever. Just to be able to talk freely, to explore difficulties and issues with these coaches, athletes and support staff was great; I appreciated what they were doing, and they appreciated my desire to create helpful conversations. It was a perfect time for reflection, usually up a mountain in a remote part of the world. It was always wonderful and I enjoyed mucking in and being eager to follow the instructions from both the head coach and team manager; we would have great banter on how effective I'd be in the British military.

I joined the team on a series of training camps in Switzerland in preparation for the World Championship in that country later that year. The setting was breathtaking, with its rolling hills and mountains, and peaceful forests. These athletes loved nothing better than a good two-hour run in terrain in the morning, followed by lunch, then another two-hour run in the afternoon. Food, massage and rest were also a vital ingredient to their preparation. The coaches would also work tremendously hard to ensure that training was planned and courses were coordinated across the forest in a designated training area.

The focus was on each athlete getting their flying hours, that is, the number of hours spent in the relevant forest terrain running and orienteering. The more hours spent doing this was vital, in building their personal databank (or 'legend') to be able to 'see' the forest at speed, as a three-dimensional picture, in order to make good decisions quickly and smoothly through each electronic control over a set number of kilometres. The team was in full swing getting ready for the World Orienteering Championships later in the year. I had already developed good relationships with the athletes and coaches and support team, and we'd discussed and planned everything; the coaches were meticulous in their detail and all elements were covered and discussed at team meetings. My role was to build the awareness of both the need for individual expertise and collective excellence with the group.

1. Awareness

In our evening workshops with the athletes, we talked about orienteering from all perspectives, their win-lose attitude to errors in the forest, and to what makes a good relay team. Our discussions were always lively. For example, some athletes spoke about the importance of winning, while others spoke about their dislike of errors; everything was discussed, including selection for specific races at specific events.

At first I was surprised by the strong opinion but as I drilled down, below the surface, I began to see some of the collective underlying emotions. In one discussion we concentrated on individual and team management of errors.

I suggested to the group: 'When is your best good enough?' This brought out a range of responses, from 'never' to 'sometimes', there were no consistent answers across the group. Most of the athletes looked puzzled and even frustrated by the question. I spoke about increasing their level of self-care as a group, and that, for me, surely their best was good enough now.

This stirred some indifferent responses. I then suggested that if their best was good enough now, they would be able to generate learning in order to find solutions as errors arose. We then had a big discussion around generating learning versus adapting to the situation. This was a very interesting debate. I highlighted the difference in terms of being proactive or reactive as a response to something uncertain. It was clear that some athletes needed convincing. This was great, I was enjoying the chance to discuss my philosophy. I asked, 'How important are errors to your work as athletes?' The response was immediate and really negative. 'We don't want to make errors', 'We don't like making errors, errors are bad'. These individuals were high achievers where there is little tolerance for making errors in every aspect of their lives; they had exceptionally high standards and had a strong value for delivering against them. Both as individuals and as a team, they perceived errors to impact their pursuit of winning; I wanted to convince them otherwise. I did this by provoking discussion on the statement: winning is for losers.

2. Belief

So we continued into the night, discussing errors in orienteering and life. I was eager to help these elite athletes learn from my lack of appreciation of errors as a young cricketer. By the next day I had put together a process for generating learning from errors for these athletes. The idea was to help them shift from a reaction to an error to a response to an error. The key to all of this was in the athletes' ability to accept the notion that their initial reaction to errors was unhealthy and selfish. This automatically created heated debate. This time they began to accept that the fear of being judged negatively was a big driver for them. We then talked about togetherness as a group and providing each other with support, especially in the relay event. They believed in each other and were a tight group. You could see and feel the freedom and enjoyment the group was having by discussing things openly. It was brilliant to hear issues that affected them both individually and as a group. The camp atmosphere was always good after one of these long healthy discussions, helping to boost the collective excellence of the group.

3. Correction

After one morning run of technical training in the terrain, we got in our cars and went down to a lake to have lunch. We sat around as a group and talked, this was a great time to reflect on what had gone on during the days before. In conjunction with the coaches we set the athletes a task, having first spelt out that we understood and accepted the dangers of a win-lose attitude, having a negative reaction to errors, and considering team selection policy issues. I gave out pieces of paper and a pen to each athlete. They had to name which squad members should be selected for which race and why. This initially created some immediate defensiveness and anxiety since they were all competing for places at the World Championships. However, because of their newfound level of openness and acceptance, they were more willing to think about what was in the best interest of the team and Great Britain.

This gave the management the opportunity to see what the athletes' thoughts were on selection. The interesting fact was that the most competitive athlete suggested that our best athlete be selected for the new sprint version of the sport. When this was announced, the other athletes agreed, however the athlete that was named disagreed, as his preference was to run the more traditional event, known as the Classic. It was discussed what was in the best interest of his team and country. This gave the head coach important feedback and a way of discussing difficult team selection issues and athlete event preferences.

He was seen as the best athlete and most thought he could do something special in the shortest form of the sport. He was not immediately impressed. It gave the coaches some useful food for thought. Being immersed in the group over significant time periods meant that the ideas and discussions went on whether it be on the team coach or over lunch or at dinner. It was always great to work with such a community who were open to thinking in a different way. What was fascinating was that because of the unique values the squad had and their desire to be consistent with these values, athletes normally competed against each other made a collective correction by selecting teams for races that gave GB the best opportunity to medal. This meant they collectively went beyond their self-interest and helped align their thoughts and feelings with the coaches. As a result, the management and coaches spent less time worrying who was in and who was out, as these major issues had already been tabled. This enabled the coaches to make the best use of all of its members and allowed our best athletes the freedom and the space to be the best that they could be.

The Defining Moment

There were two defining moments. First, the athlete chosen by the athletes and coaches to run the new event in world orienteering became GB's first ever world champion for the sprint race – a surprise for the athlete as well as the entire squad and management. The new Great Britain world champion had learnt much about himself and his team. During the sprint race he made the mistake of not taking the most optimal route from Control Three to Control Four but, over this period, he had become more accepting of his errors and, as a result, was able to maintain his focus and composure. This meant that he relaxed and increased his thoughts on how to master his route choices for the rest of the race. This led him to strategically plan ahead, choosing the right route choice at Control Ten. He said, 'You might not run the perfect race but you have to spike each control perfectly,' in reference to making mistakes but using the mistakes to generate learning.

Our new world champion, when interviewed on TV, expressed his total surprise at winning, suggesting to the presenter, 'I was just concentrating on my race . . . I had no hope of winning.' (This phrase has since become a mantra amongst all those who follow the Leadership withoutEGO® philosophy.)

He also made reference to his change of perspective following a mistake. This athlete had a history of compounding one error with another; he and I spent significant time talking about responding to errors rather than reacting to them. As a result, our GB world champion had a complete shift in thinking when faced with an error during his race. The concept of appreciating errors became a big element of British orienteering success and his leadership within the relay team.

 27. STOP: LOOK: LISTEN

'I was just concentrating on my race . . . I had no hope of winning' –

What can you do to develop a similar attitude of concentration and no hope of winning?

Does it feel strange to hold a 'no hope of winning' attitude?

Second, the three-man relay team talked more about their relationships both in their team and in the squad and how they could improve things. One thought was to break out of their established roles within the team, giving greater energy and commitment to each member of the team. Such openness and sharing made the collective excellence of the group even stronger, not only within the relay teams (both men and women) but the entire group. The squad found that if they could realign what they thought about winning for the team and their pure love for being the best at what they do then they could achieve more, which they did. Several other nations were interested in understanding our team methodology. Fittingly, the GB men's team won a bronze medal in the World Orienteering Relay Race and a few years later the men's team went on to win gold to become Orienteering Relay World Champions.

 28. STOP: LOOK: LISTEN

How does it feel to share in someone else's success?

What do you learn about yourself through the success of others?

Can you immediately celebrate the success of those around you?

Your ABC Plan: Appreciating Your Errors

You need to think about what your errors tell you about yourself. Are you filled with self-criticism when you make a mistake? Or do you appreciate your errors?

If you have answered 'yes' to the first question you have a big problem. I believe any form of criticism is terrible for us, while self-criticism is even worse as it unwittingly induces even more emotional turmoil. Our self-esteem is built on evidence that we can do something well. If we don't get the outcome evidence our self-esteem suffers, and we come crashing down, unable to cope with the emotional pain errors trigger. We feel like a failure. We tell ourselves negative and critical things.

Errors are perceived like thorns in our sides, constantly giving us pain and scrutiny. We are taught not to like making mistakes. The people around us, including all forms of media, place an extraordinary pressure on us to look right, perform right and achieve right. Mistakes are not accepted. As a result, we are tasked with pushing those winning margins with an absolute desire to go harder, faster and stronger in all we do as winning margins become smaller. The level of intensity is suffocating. I have witnessed many leaders across a wide spectrum push for no-error environments only to see their performers completely derailed by it. The 'no room for errors' mandate achieves the exact opposite by making mistakes easier. We begin to live life on the edge, feeling very uncomfortable and less likely that we can perform.

Instead, we need to learn to embrace our errors. We must begin to develop a blind faith regarding our ability and not constantly seek evidence that we are either good or bad at something. We need to understand that real failure only occurs when we stop breathing!

Having blind faith requires you to accept your shortcomings and errors. By doing this you automatically stop the emotional spiral of errors and the psychological wounds and pain that come along with them. That is, one error being followed by another error and the cycle goes on. It takes tremendous flexibility to tolerate errors and to see them as building blocks to your future success. This builds and protects your emotional resilience. Here you need to learn how to appreciate yourself following errors at something important. Showing self-compassion is vital if gains are to be made. Here you will generate learning from errors by embracing what the experience of errors has to offer. Smiling at errors is key to your success.

It might be, for example, a teacher assessing a child's errors or a sports coach (or support team) critically appraising an athlete or a boss analysing staff mistakes. The negative feedback means we pay too much attention to 'what is wrong with me?' kind of thinking. This is toxic and dangerous. Instead, all these individuals need to smile and accept the learning coming from the situation, seeing their position in all that is said and done. This only adds to our deepening pressure in life that getting things right and winning is the only choice.

For example, the onset of the Internet and social media has made matters worse. How we are seen throughout social media is now a matter of winning or losing.

 29. STOP: LOOK: LISTEN

What is your social media presence online?

Do you feel the pressure to keep up appearances with others online?

Have you made social media mistakes?

This constant attention on whether we are seen as a winner or loser is affecting all of us from a pupil to a mum to an executive to an athlete. We are unable to switch off and this unlimited access leads to significant errors in life. Social media has magnified the critical judgement of others who feel free to say what they thinking. I don't want to make light of this huge area of concern by only giving it a brief insight here. All stakeholders – including parents, schools, businesses, churches and local authorities – need to pay greater attention to providing adequate discussion and research to chart a way forward.

ABC Plan – 'Appreciating Your Errors'

Aligning your attitudes, behaviour, values and beliefs

So, by working through your own Awareness, Belief and Correction (ABC) Plan you will be in a better position to see how your appreciation of errors impacts on your life.

Awareness (A): Error Attitude

You will need to examine your attitude towards errors in life. Do you agree or disagree that errors are good for you while you hunt winning at something? How aware are you of your errors in life? If you are unaware of your errors, you will most definitely be operating with self-importance or selfishly.

Belief (B): Error Behaviour

You will need to assess your error behaviour. Do you ignore your errors with significant people while you are doing something important? Are you able to accept your error behaviour in life? If you ignore your errors, you are almost certainly functioning with self-importance or selfishly.

Correction (C): Error Values and Beliefs

You will need to consider what your underlying values and beliefs are about things you dream about and fear in life? You will need to consider how you can align your attitudes, behaviours, values and beliefs in order to embrace your errors in life. If you choose to cultivate an ABC Plan you will actively seek to understand errors in your life. This is an essential self-correction needed to shift your values and beliefs towards winning for the benefit of others. The aim of this process is to shift from a winning for oneself (selfish) to winning for others (selfless) perspective. This will give you a deeper level of joy and contentment.

The pursuit of winning for others increases the likelihood of you being open to align your attitude, behaviour, values and beliefs about dealing with the uncomfortable truths in the way you win and lose in life.

You need to spend some time thinking about aligning your thoughts and feelings. So, instead of thinking about winning for one's self, think about winning for others – a community, school, club, or country. How does that make you feel? Does it feel different to thinking about winning for one's self?

It is always great to see people take this journey as they begin to truly see how selfish attitudes and behaviours occur as they pursue winning. They learn to accept winning for one's self has a negative effect on their life. Individuals may or may not see these attitudes reflecting their core values and beliefs. It is fantastic to see people take up the challenge of thinking, feeling and acting better as they align their attitude, behaviour, values and beliefs from a selfless or giving to others perspective.

I had the privilege of working with a Great Britain

orienteer who was an exceptional elite athlete. She had the focus, determination and attention to detail to climb to world-class standard over many years. However, it wasn't enough. She dreamt of becoming a world champion. She was eager to learn from her errors and find her true authenticity as an elite athlete, believing it would come through becoming a world champion. She began to accept that she needed to be more understanding of her errors with both her orienteering and other people in the team. She began to process her feelings and negative attitude and behaviour towards other specific members of the team. She was able to gain greater awareness of how to align her values and beliefs. For example, she began to process her conflict with another world-class athlete and why it occurred. She was able to see her contribution to her poor relationship with this athlete and how it was negatively impacting on the team and the staff. Awareness and acceptance of this error meant things began to change. As a result, she began to explore how to achieve winning through processing her error avoidance. She also began to consider her contribution to Great Britain and world orienteering and how she could yield a greater and more positive influence on others. Over the years, she became increasingly keen to think about how she could offer something back to her community.

Through her ability and desire to self-correct her attitude towards specific individuals, she became freer and happier. As a result, she immersed herself in mastering her skills and technique and cultivating her desire to make a difference to the team by resolving a long-held conflict position with another team member. By seeing her errors with others more clearly she was able to fulfil her true world-class talent on the biggest stage in her sport. Her perception of what success looked like began to shift. She began to think about what impact she was having on others. She went from worrying what others thought to achieving her life-long dream of winning a medal at the World Championship. Today, she is passing on her experiences as an executive coach, helping others to be aware of who they are and how to get the best from their potential.

This example highlights her ability to align attitude and behaviour with values and beliefs. She was able to shift from high levels of defensiveness, self-absorption and fear to a more open and appreciative view of her errors. She became even more inspirational to others both in her team and around the world. She became an even better role model by appreciating her errors more. As a result, she significantly moved away from a tendency to think of success in terms of working harder, faster and stronger on just her orienteering to understanding that working on her way of thinking was the final piece of the jigsaw puzzle for achieving her dreams at the World Championships.

In conclusion, how you react or respond to errors has a massive impact on whether others choose to follow you or not. Do you agree? Your reaction or response to errors indicates your level of selfishness versus selflessness.

Do you agree? When you self-correct conflict errors with others, how does it make you feel?

What are your examples of self-correcting your errors in your life?

ABC Plan Summary

In Step One, you pressed your own TV remote control on how you go about winning in life; what did the data reveal? Now you must begin the process of appreciating your errors by answering the following questions:

I want you to think about as many examples as you can where you have been very self-critical following an error with either your performance or with your relationships with others. For example, think about some of the biggest mistakes you have made in life – what were they?

Write them down. What was your level of self-criticism? How did it feel?

Now for every example of self-criticism I want you to transform it into a more self-appreciative statement of your mistake. That is, take some time to consider what you can appreciate about your error – what learning can you generate as a result of making the error?

Write your error appreciation. What was your level of self-appreciation? How did it feel?

Step Two: Appreciating Errors
What is the main difference between the two lists? Show the lists to a family member or friend and discuss how you have learnt about how self-critical you are. Discover

also what you appreciate about yourself. What can you accept about your errors?

What do you take away from doing this activity? Why do you ignore your errors? What time can you allocate to self-correction of your mistakes? How can responding appreciatively to errors inspire others?

Regardless of whether you are playing sport or in business or education or simply at home with your family, hunting winning increases the likelihood that we will become blind to seeing our errors in life, whether they be internal with one's self or external conflict with others. Our ego takes over, especially when the pressure is on. What errors can you self-correct under pressure? What do you tell yourself? What you tell yourself is your ego. In appreciating errors you must learn to enjoy generating learning from your mistakes. Does making errors make you more selfish in what you do?

What are your thoughts on the following questions?

- What was your initial response or reaction to such an activity and the error questions?
- Was it difficult to assess errors? Did it make you feel uncomfortable? Or did you want to seek answers?
- Does it feel uncomfortable to focus on yourself?
- What do you most become aware of about your errors?
- Did thinking about your mistakes trigger any discomfort? Or was it an enjoyable activity?
- What are your uncomfortable truths about your mistakes in life?
- What do your emotions tell you about the way you

either ignore or process mistakes?

- Were you able to see your mistakes from a new perspective?
- What did you discover about your ego in relation to your errors?
- Did you enjoy or dislike taking time to stop, look and listen to your mistakes?

Smile Mindfulness

Imagine a world full of self-appreciation and no self-criticism. Over Step Two, I want you to focus on celebrating your errors in life and what you have learnt from them. In fact, appreciating your errors and finding a way to make the most of them is key to increasing your happiness. Now, I want you to record how it feels to increase your acceptance and self-correct a typical response to mistakes in your life. Keep a mood diary to chart how you are feeling, putting a smiling face indicating that you have embraced your errors and a sad face indicating that it was difficult to embrace your errors. Once you have some good data consider the following questions:

1. *Did any pattern emerge from showing more appreciation of your errors?*
2. *Do you experience any satisfaction from changing how you responded to your errors?*
3. *What impact did embracing your errors have on those around you?*
4. *What errors did you consistently repeat and why?*

5. *What was your method of self-correcting an error?*

6. *How many smiling faces did you record in the week and what does it mean? Equally, how many sad faces did you record in the week and what does it mean?*

7. *Did you share your appreciating errors activity with anyone else? If yes, what did you learn about appreciating your errors from discussing it with others? Do you think there is any benefit to continuing the exercise over the coming weeks, months or years?*

So, which way does your coin end up? Do you focus on self-criticism? Or did you embrace your mistakes? Of course we all like to think we can think positively about our errors but it is indeed difficult. However, I have discovered that appreciating all you do including your errors is the best way of inspiring others to do the same. I have many experiences of how the appreciation of errors created momentum for everyone, not just the person making the mistake. Their positive response to a mistake reduced fear and helped others get the most from what they were doing. Embracing both internal and external error conflict is something the best in the world do intuitively. You must groove the appreciation of your errors in order to fulfil your potential and operate more selflessly. Self-criticism puts us into a selfish mode and leads to long-term negative health consequences.

Please select which statement best reflects you when you are about to do something important in life: '*I get so angry at making mistakes,*' or '*I can accept my mistakes.*'

Choice 1. 'I get so angry at making mistakes'

Self-critical mind-set: Focusing on self-criticism is ego (self-importance) driven. It places our attention on a negative view of ourselves. You will enter a world of unhappiness. Here your aim is to be self-critical before others start to negatively judge you. You start to feel better as the self-criticism deflects you away from the reality of your error. Your errors make you feel really bad. In fact, a first mistake is followed by a second that is followed by a third and so on. You experience high levels of stress and burnout as your mistakes drain you. You work hard to resolve your errors but still feel discomfort from making them. Quality performances are inconsistent. Your confidence is affected by the constant flow of errors. Your high level of self-criticism means you take no time for reflection. You feel incredibly judged by others.

Choice 2. 'I can accept my mistakes'

Accepting errors mind-set: Focusing on accepting your errors is without ego driven. You are eager to generate learning from your mistakes. You are open to what your mistakes are telling you. You are not self-critical as you are focused on how learning from your mistakes can help your team or community. You see the bigger picture regarding what impact you can have on your community. You get immense pleasure out of learning from your errors. You smile at your mistakes as you fully accept that they are part of your performance and life. You are able to inform others of your learning that inspires them to think differently of their own mistakes. They also begin to understand that it is key to learn from mistakes rather than simply just focusing on winning. There is a greater appreciation of responding in the right way to mistakes. You are excited by the challenge of each error you make. Errors are perceived as natural and you accept they are part of your journey and performance. You gain immense joy out of generating learning from mistakes.

Conclusion

How does it feel to observe yourself when your make a mistake from a mindfulness perspective? What is your psychological and physical reaction to an error? What do errors say about you? The more self-observation of your self-criticism the better you will be at dealing with adversity in life. Elite athletes, executives, students and parents became more creative once they were able to talk through their errors and potential solutions to them. They truly began to see the joy in the prospect of generating learning from mistakes.

Greater acceptance of our errors and associated behaviour leads to greater satisfaction and autonomy, which in turn leads to greater freedom and happiness. Here the individual gets immersed in deep learning from errors and as a result is able to execute a greater performance. The fear of being criticised, judged or rejected has been minimised and the person can slowly start to restore their mental wellbeing.

19

STEP THREE: Do You Take Time Finding Out What You Avoid?

• • •

The third step to detox your ego is to answer the above question.

If you answer yes, you're headed in the right direction to being free of your ego and happier in life. Being an open vessel to difficult things or situations in your life is key to operating without ego. If, however, your immediate reaction is no, then you are running on ego. Here you will attempt to pursue winning for yourself. Being closed to winning for others is dangerous and must change. Taking time to see what you 'avoid' is the third characteristic of ego and it shows how emotional pain is hidden in life. You will see how avoidance is a selfish act in life.

This step enables you to explore your initial data arising from Step One and Step Two. For example, do you want to win at any cost? Or, do you find it difficult to accept losing? Taking time to see what your data really says is key to reducing your ego response. By doing this you can begin to understand how self-centred you are. You can also begin to think about how others can benefit from your approach to winning. You will see how avoidance is an ego response. You need to develop a softness towards avoidance so that you can understand it and self-correct. Building resilience in your life by being softer towards your avoidance is a difficult and time-consuming process.

Your journey starts with a coin flip and a choice.

time

Time Choice

Whether you know it or not, when you flip your coin of *time* you have a choice to make. You choose either a 'closed' or 'open' mind-set. Whichever side your coin lands on will trigger a self-fulfilling prophecy. That is, you will either take the time to focus on avoidance or openness in your life.

So, if you are closed to taking time to discover what you avoid in your life, you are choosing an ego reaction. You are choosing to pay attention to fear in your life. This is characterised by the statement: *'I've got no time to look at what I avoid.'* Clearly, such a reaction means you are in fact avoiding some uncomfortable truths in your life. Being closed means you will limit your freedom, happiness and success in life.

However, if you are open to taking the time to look at what you avoid, you are choosing a selfless response as you begin to find a way to be even more helpful to your community. You are choosing to pay attention to joy in your life. This takes courage and is characterised by the statement: *'I am open to all things; even though it is difficult and uncomfortable to talk about, I'm prepared to take the time'.*

By definition, elite athletes who cross the line and become world champions are, at this defining moment, taking time to look at what they avoid. Here, they are free, happy and ready for success in life.

---

 30. STOP: LOOK: LISTEN

What do you avoid in life?

Are you willing and committed to stop, look and listen to your internal traffic regarding what you avoid in your pursuit of winning in your life?

My Personal Experience of Avoidance

During my first class county cricket debut I refused to look at what I was avoiding, especially when my performance started to decline. I felt under a microscope. Everything I did was magnified and I felt judged. I tried to ignore it. I had just become a full-time pro and I felt a huge pressure to deliver a high performance. These changes were subtle and intangible from four weeks earlier when I made my second eleven county debut. I was totally unaware of how my ego was impacting me. Instead, I chose to focus intently on what I had to do. Unfortunately, I wasn't aware that by doing this I was becoming too self-absorbed and self-centred. Put simply I was being drawn into a selfish act of performing for myself. For example, I remember dropping some high catches in practice before the start of the match, creating a few jokes and some banter with my teammates. This made me feel terrible, but I chose to ignore the emotional pain of this moment. Instead, I buried it away from my thoughts.

These buried feelings returned as the match started and I opened the bowling, only to be torn apart by two international cricketers at the peak of their skills. I delivered a poor performance. I was devastated and tried to put on a brave face when I actually felt like I was drowning inside. It was awful.

Can you think of a time in your life where you had a similar experience of choking at something?

Like a lot of individuals in sport, business and life, I chose to fight my initial thoughts and feelings in an attempt to make a better fist of it. It was like a war and I was fighting to survive and needed to be tough. I chose to disregard the emotional torment and pain the experience generated. I refused to see what was really happening inside. Such avoidance significantly increased my stress levels, which further heightened my situation and added to my distraction and poor performance. I was clearly paying attention to the fear of the situation without even knowing it. I also completely ignored the fact that my dream of playing first class cricket was becoming my nightmare. I ignored the uncomfortable truth that I wasn't fulfilling my potential. I was completely blind to why I didn't feel the same as I did four weeks earlier. What had changed? My technique hadn't so what was that 'something missing' element? I simply didn't have the emotional awareness to understand my internal traffic. I wasn't open to understanding what was really making me feel uncomfortable.

When I first qualified as a psychologist I was eager to help others learn from my inconsistent performance by paying attention to fear instead of focusing on the joy of the moment.

 31. STOP: LOOK: LISTEN

Can you think of any occasion, sport, activity or social gathering where you feared being negatively judged by others?

What could you have done to embrace such negative judgement?

By examining what you avoid, you can really start to unearth your own selfishness. At the heart of human avoidance is a selfish desire to prevent emotional pain. This captures more of our thoughts than our desire to seek out pleasure.

I am always surprised at the level of avoidance successful individuals and teams ooze. I have worked with and held many discussions with international sports stars from the world of cricket, football, golf, snooker, athletics, orienteering and diving. I've found that the more successful an individual or team is, the more likely they are to ignore some of the uncomfortable truths in their lives. Their winning becomes so intoxicating that it leads to being a hindrance to seeing their own personal truth. Their success blinds their ability to see things they are obviously ducking. The first time I noticed this it was puzzling as I assumed their high level of success was an indicator of greater freedom and happiness in life. In my mind, avoidance was soon becoming a major problem for those who win and become successful.

When I first started to work with pro cricketers, I found they would ignore the same things I ignored as a player. I would welcome the opportunity to highlight this which created further discussion and the player would walk away feeling much better even though at times there were no solutions. Just the opportunity to talk was great for these individuals. When I got the chance to work and talk with international cricketers from various different countries I was again taken aback that they too had stories and experiences that avoided some obvious truths. It has been particularly satisfying to get international cricketers who are supposed to be in competition with one another to share their thoughts about the demands of the game at a world level and delivering high performance. Competition invokes a win or lose attitude (see the next step), which leads to greater avoidance. This is very harmful to us as described in Step One.

In these situations, I am always on the lookout to encourage individuals to become more open and softer than they ordinarily want to be. I wanted them to share with their competitors what makes them anxious and fearful. This is always an interesting and revealing process that leads to greater gains for all when they eventually perform against each other. They appear freer as they emotionally shift away from *'it's all about me'* to understanding *'it's all about my team'*. Being more selfless builds resilience. Something I found difficult to do. They gained an appreciation of their ambassadorial role in the world game. They learned to see their role in performing for their country and as a result increased their ability to inspire others. They began to see a much bigger purpose for delivering performance that went beyond themselves. They began to see competition differently. Instead of competing to beat their opponent, they get immersed in how their performance can inspire their nation. They become more open to thinking it's not just about winning. They cultivate their beliefs and values about what their contribution is to the game worldwide. They have gone beyond their sport. Their new frame of reference is 'it's all about winning for my community', be it team, country or world.

Getting two international cricketers from different countries sharing their experiences and fears of high-level cricket was amazing. Both agreed it was different and slightly exposing to reveal things but it opened up the possibility of learning new things. Importantly, it gave them both a chance to share things about their new experiences in international cricket. They were able to bring to the surface some of their concerns from many different perspectives. They were able to open up and talk about things they would otherwise keep to themselves. They both agreed it was good to speak and see competition through a new lens of custodians of the game. Such enlightening experiences enabled them to gain even greater freedom and happiness at the most intense moments of international cricket. I use the notion of 'sharing with your competition' as a check of where the individual sits in terms of selfishness and selflessness. I have seen many performers across lots of sports share more with those that they are competing with. Performers understand immediately the benefits of not avoiding how competition makes them feel. This is a good thing as it builds resilience. Interestingly, these two international cricketers performed unbelievably well for their respective countries during the various Test matches. Both have achieved outstanding match-winning performances. I have also experienced avoidance in many different workplace environments. Below is an example of a business that was committed and willing to give time to look at avoidance within their recruitment process in order to help select the right candidates into the right positions.

Avoidance in Business – a Correction

I have enjoyed helping executives to face the avoidance question. I've had many discussions with executives about what they avoid in life. Sometimes I'm faced with complete denial and defensiveness. At other times, it stimulates lots of discussion and debate. I can immediately see which executives are sufficiently open to their emotional pain by the way they explore avoidance in life. Helping executives understand what they avoid is always tough. It is always encouraging when organisations, both in sport and business, take up the challenge of looking at avoidance during the selection and recruitment process. I was very fortunate to work with a vice-president at a global IT company who had the vision and foresight to see the benefit of understanding avoidance within his business unit.

The Recruitment, Induction, Performance Excellence (RIPE) process helps organisations to understand how to identify, select and develop the right people, in the right roles, executing the right performance for their organisations. This process allows them to provide a development plan from the outset of their appointment. Here, candidates are assessed and monitored on all the characteristics of ego in order to ensure person-environment fit. The avoidance question has particular relevance as it assesses the level of candidate openness and flexibility. It is always very interesting to see an organisation take up the challenge of building the criteria of ego assessment into their recruitment process.

It has also been fascinating to see an organisation's initial reaction to the concept of avoidance. Over the years, I have had people, in both sport and business, completely reject it, while others have been eager to know more and want to explore it further. It is always fantastic to see organisations take up the challenge of assessing candidate ego at recruitment stage and then being able to build a process to develop the new hire at the outset of their appointment. This is refreshing as there is a clear meeting of minds between the organisation and new hire. It also quickly unravels where there is no match between candidate and manager. I have seen, on many occasions, candidates simply de-select themselves from the process as these characteristics of ego entered the discussion.

In terms of candidates, observable avoidance behaviour is seen. This gives an indication of the emotional world of each candidate. The question of avoidance gives the recruiter a window into candidate data on what they hide.

 32. STOP: LOOK: LISTEN

If you were on a selection interview, what would you say to the question: what do you avoid?

How does it make you feel?

I'm still surprised by how candidates answer this question. Do they react or respond to it? Do they smile or appear awkward in response to the question? How does their avoidance attitude and behaviour manifest in the interview process? Are candidates free and open or do they appear stuck? These are interesting questions that give a clear indication of each candidate's hidden world of emotional pain. As a result, it reveals their developmental needs straight away. This means the organisation can design their induction process to include supporting each developmental area for the new hires. In this way, weaker areas in emotional terms can be identified and a planned process of change can be implemented at the outset of their appointment. This helps align both the candidate to the organisation and the organisation to the candidate, resulting in greater concentration on delivering excellence in their role. Here the meeting of minds between the new hires and hiring manager ensures fears about the role are addressed openly from the beginning. I have found the new hires will find creative ways to perform as they begin to feel free and alive in the role. High performance will be achieved. In contrast, below is an example of how avoidance can impact freedom and happiness in a student's exam preparation.

Avoidance in Student Life

I have had countless experiences of consulting with students who, while approaching important exams, get into episodes of avoidance. Here they appear stressed, anxious and full of concern about what might or might not happen. The big question at this time is:

What does the stress and anxiety tell you about what you are avoiding?

This always invokes a strong reaction, as a student's

natural desire is to avoid being asked about what they are avoiding in their situation. To them the easy answer to avoidance is to say that it's all about the examination pressure and how to handle it. While on the surface, this may be true, below the surface something else is happening. When I speak to them in this way, it captures their attention and they tend to calm down, wanting to hear a deeper explanation to understanding their stress reaction and so we begin to explore the issues.

For example, an A-level student came to me worried, unhappy and anxious. I gave him time and space to describe what was happening to him. He was clearly stressed and frustrated with exam deadlines approaching and too much work to do. This stress manifested itself in a number of incidents. First, he managed to tip a bottle of water over his computer while he was revising, sending him and his machine into meltdown. Second, while trying to take a break he managed to smash a window with his basketball. Finally, he was having numerous arguments with his siblings. I asked him to consider what he was avoiding. Initially he was taken aback by the question and I could clearly see him getting ready to defend himself although he was silent and unsure about how to answer it.

So, I asked him the same question but in a different way. What do you think your incidents represent? He then described the typical, standard reply of examination and time pressure in a home that was pretty noisy and distracting. He spoke about his siblings with a mild degree of irritation and frustration, citing the noise level as a major obstacle to studying.

After his outpouring of frustration about what was stressing him, I returned to the initial line of enquiry that this stress was representing something else. What? He started to think much more deeply about what I was asking him. He began to talk about how his exams were more an indication of how he felt regarding being compared within his peer group. It became clear that it wasn't about his ability to be tested under pressure; instead, it was about being compared to a peer group of high achievers. His began to see his fear about whether he would still be included in the group if he got a series of poor results. How would he be compared to this group? What would his teachers and parents say if he fell short of his peer group comparison? It became clear that his greatest fear was that he wouldn't do as well as other members of this group and this thought was devastating to him. We spent time talking through how it felt being positioned as the weakest member of this top group. We specifically outlined worst-case scenarios by asking: what if you failed every exam? What would be the worst that could happen? 'Re-sit them or I could be something else,' he replied.

We dug deeper into his need to compare himself to this top group of boys in his school. Why? I asked. Why is it so important to feel in with this group? He had no real explanation. He agreed that it wasn't healthy and that it was largely irrelevant what others did but he felt it necessary to compare his talents to that of others in the group. I again asked: why? And again he didn't have an answer.

It was a really interesting exchange and I was eager to keep probing further. It was clear that his stress was not about his competence in sitting his examinations. It wasn't about whether he was good enough. Instead, it was about feeling a sense of belonging within this top group. He didn't want to fall out of membership to this group. The thought of being rejected from the group was more stressful than actually sitting the series of papers. This discovery was a huge realisation that what he had been telling himself wasn't true or accurate. I asked him what it felt like to be positioned at the centre of this group. You could see the stress simply ebb away. He immediately felt much better and able to concentrate on his revision as he accepted that the source of his stress wasn't sitting the exams. Instead, he was able to make the necessary self-correction in what he chose to tell himself in his emotional world. It became clear that he had a greater appreciation of the true cause and effect of his stress, attitude and behaviour.

As a result, he decided to make a number of changes. First, he decided that there was no benefit to what he was telling himself and so he immediately stopped thinking about his exams in an anxious way. This allowed him to plan more excitedly about his exam execution. This resulted in him moving to his grandparent's house a few days before each of his big examinations in order to do his final preparations. The quiet and peaceful environment allowed him to get immersed in his revision and sustain his relationships with his siblings. Finally, he had the benefit of being able to celebrate his knowledge of his subject matter with his grandparents, which made the night before his exams joyful. In conclusion, he was able to generate a deeper understanding of his anxiety and stress by looking at what he was avoiding. He gained an insight into the uncomfortable truth that his exams represented a fear of being excluded from his peer group.

What do you learn from this example?

I have used his example to highlight how the individual was able to make a significant change in aligning his thinking and action to achieve more. This individual became aware of how avoidance impacted his pursuit of winning in his life. Such examples highlight our overt self-importance or selfishness as we begin to ignore things that are harmful.

My ABC Example:
A World Champion Kickboxer

This is an outline example of an ABC Plan for a world champion, highlighting how an individual was able to make a significant change in aligning his thinking and action to achieve more. This individual became aware of how avoidance impacted the pursuit of winning in his life at the moment of 'crossing the line' in a world championship final. This example highlights our self-interest as we begin to create a harmful strong internal expectation to win.

A world-class kickboxer asked for my help to achieve a lifetime's dream of becoming a world champion in what he perceived as the most difficult kickboxing world organisation – World Association of Kickboxing Organisation (WAKO). He had reached breaking point. He had five previous attempts to win a world title within this organisation. He was an exceptional elite athlete, with superior fitness, athleticism and a decorated career with numerous world titles. He had won almost everything over his career. His normal way of working was to go harder, faster and stronger to achieve exceptional performance in his sport. However, he was frustrated at not being able to understand why he couldn't achieve the success within the WAKO World Championship. He decided to take time with me to explore it further.

1: Awareness

My aim was to help him see his situation from a very different perspective. We began by discussing the two competing statements. Which statement best reflected his approach: *'I don't really avoid anything'* or, *'I am open to all things, even though it is difficult and uncomfortable to talk about'?*

He was beginning to embrace being open regarding his under-performance at the WAKO World Championship, as he was puzzled and frustrated about why there was so much of a marked difference between this and other world championship events. What was stopping him perform with consistency at WAKO? What was he not seeing in his approach to WAKO? These were new questions to him and he admitted to struggling to find answers. He had never needed to ask himself such questions, but the context of his situation demanded it. He was at a new level that required a deeper sense of self-awareness.

We had many deep discussions about these questions and I tried to foster a spirit of reflection regarding what he was avoiding in the context of becoming a WAKO world champion. We spent some time looking at all his world title success and comparing it to his unsuccessful attempts at WAKO. A distinct pattern started to emerge. He began to see that he thought and felt very differently during a WAKO event compared to other world events. It took some time for him to appreciate and understand how his way of thinking was contributing to his lack of success. We explored each of his five attempts at becoming a world champion in greater detail. This was a difficult process, as he naturally became defensive and resistant to the probing and drilling down into his avoidance behaviour. It was amazing to see him develop greater flexibility about his action under pressure, and how he began to see how his rhythm and flow was being affected by his overwhelming desire to win a WAKO world title. Open discussion about his deep need to win WAKO revealed how out of control he felt about winning it. This was a new experience for him. We took time to explore his new situation and context, looking at how his frustration from the mismatch between his level of expertise or mastery and the results in WAKO heavily impacted his self-esteem and confidence.

This drove his desire to win so much that his attitudes and behaviours became all about him. He became too self-absorbed. He would work harder, faster and stronger in order to ensure he would cross the line first. Each failure would lead him to working even more intensely to find a solution. Nothing worked. After failing at five attempts he became open to doing something different.

He found this hard to reconcile and it caused tremendous stress. He lost fights he should have won. He became increasingly tense at the slightest talk of what he was missing in his preparation for WAKO. He found it difficult to express himself freely. This awareness building was essential for him to develop a solution. We explored how he could find a way to accept that he may never win a title within this organisation due to what he was avoiding. This was a very uncomfortable moment for him. This was tough for him to consider. Below the surface, it was clear that his values and beliefs about his level of skills as a world-class kickboxer didn't match his attitude and behaviour at WAKO. We needed to understand more and unravel what he was blind to.

2: Belief

Therefore, on the surface, he was feeling negatively judged due to not being able to win the most coveted prize in world kickboxing. While below the surface, he was unintentionally paying attention to the feelings of not being fully valued by his peers when fighting within WAKO competitions. As a fighter he was choosing to be less effective. This was a great realisation: it became clear that he was blocking the very thing he wanted to feel strong and powerful for. Why? I asked. He didn't know, he couldn't see what it was. 'Do you need evidence of being world-class?', I asked. He immediately said, 'Yes'. I was taken aback by this, suggesting he had all the evidence in the world that he was world-class. He replied, 'Maybe, but not in the WAKO organisation.' I asked him, 'Does this reveal something deeper about your drive to be judged as a world champion in this organisation?' 'Yes, this is very important to me,' he replied. I then asked him whether he felt competent enough, and he said 'yes'. He expanded that if he retired not winning a world title in a WAKO event he wouldn't get the respect he wanted from others. He wouldn't get the reverence from the world of elite kickboxing.

He immediately started to see and accept his own part in his under-performance in WAKO. He was beginning to realise that there was a mismatch between what he was telling himself and his fantastic kickboxing results at world level. I asked him to explain what was really going on. He began to explore it and an excitement started to appear as I asked him to think about the respect those within WAKO gave him. He expanded on the others who had won at WAKO as well as the WAKO officials and spectators. I asked him to show me how all those individuals respected him. He began to list lots and lots of reasons why he was respected at world level. I asked him what it felt like to be respected by so many.

This was a life-changing line of enquiry, as he began to see the possibilities of accepting that he had been looking at this from a closed perspective. He accepted he needed to be open about his avoidance regarding respect and to bin the pattern of thinking and behaving that suggested this was an issue of fear of rejection. This was a freeing experience where all his previous pain of underperformance in WAKO provided a platform for developing something new. Unearthing his deep-seated need to win WAKO to gain respect from others was overwhelming. He realised his ambassadorial role in the sport and that he was at the heart of the sport. He needed to think about how he could inspire the next generation of kick-boxers. This was an interesting and soul-searching experience that helped formulate a self-correction plan for his next venture into the WAKO World Championships.

 33. STOP: LOOK: LISTEN

Where can you become an ambassador in life?

What do you have to do differently to become more valued by others?

3: Correction

With this newfound awareness and acceptance he began the process of self-correction. How could he begin to accept that he had the respect already and needed to use this to contribute to the GB team by the way he fought at WAKO? By asking him to think about how winning could benefit others you could see the immediate reduction in his anxiety about his fixation regarding WAKO. This feeling of being able to identify the cause and effect underlying what he told himself was great insight for him to create change. He instantly understood what he chose to tell himself regarding rejection. Instead, he began to have absolute blind faith in his ability to execute his skills at the WAKO Championships by feeling that he had the respect of significant others.

This immediately changed our discussions about his preparation for the championships as his energy and enthusiasm increased. We discussed what would make him feel strong and invincible throughout the WAKO World Championship. With our work together he learned to accept that he needed to change his view of himself in his sport.

This was a massive step to build a plan of self-correction regarding his sixth WAKO attempt. We began talking about all of his success in the sport and the level of recognition he had around the world. He began to realise that while it was nice to win the WAKO title it wasn't everything. He accepted that he could lose, but that he was happy with what he had achieved in his sport. He felt more uplifted and free, and developed a need to understand more deeply his contribution to his sport, from a leadership and mentoring perspective. He began to appreciate there was a greater role the sport required from him other that his self-absorption in yet another world title. In these discussions, winning a title had less emphasis as we talked about helping the GB team learn how to express themselves freely on the world level.

We began to talk about finding a Special Place where he felt totally respected, free and alive. He became enlightened and full of energy when he stopped thinking about being judged in the eyes of others. Instead he began to explore his very own Special Place where he felt most respected, free and not judged. In this place, he stopped avoiding his real fear of being rejected by individuals within the WAKO organisation. He became acutely aware of his status in the sport that had been validated by his success over many years. He was happy to generate learning about what approach to take with his latest world championship by using blind faith of his kickboxing mastery. This allowed him to really think about how he was going to achieve his ultimate dream. He became aware that his deep level of self-absorption that had taken him to world-class level and helped him win other world championship titles was an inhibitor for him to win at WAKO.

He developed a new way of looking at what he had avoided whilst chasing the WAKO title. Winning WAKO was about gaining perceived respect from others and being judged more positively. When he realised that this was a selfish act, he immediately began to feel free. In his Special Place he felt a surge of energy and inspiration to express himself freely. He understood he had a chance to become a true ambassador for the sport – a more selfless perspective. As a result, he attuned to not needing evidence and accepted blind faith in his ability. This allowed him to shift his thinking away from self-centredness to thinking how his kickboxing mastery could help Great Britain's fighters (and fighters around the world) be inspired by his approach. This seemed to energise him and free him from worry. He was able to 'get out of the way' of himself. He began to imagine what his fighting would do to the GB team. He instantly became happier, freer and ready for the competition. His new selfless mind-set steered him through each round and into the final. His typical high level of stress was replaced with a calm authority of readiness, capability and rhythm. He soon realised that being out of control gave him the control he needed to succeed. He enjoyed taking control of his situation by being able to showcase his skills for the benefit of others. As a result, his normal rhythm and grace returned in the most important world championship of his career.

The Defining Moment

He progressed through to the final and ended up winning it comprehensively, becoming the WAKO World Champion. He had finally found a way to freely express his undoubted ability. His newfound way of thinking to fight beyond himself had enabled him to focus on how he could inspire others and in so doing, he gave himself the best chance to perform freely and achieve his long-held dream.

Your ABC Plan: Finding a 'Special Place' in Your Life

Being able to find a 'Special Place' so that you can stop and have a high degree of stillness and freedom to do nothing except think is a difficult task to achieve.

What are your immediate thoughts – do you take 'time' for reflection? Or do you have 'no time' for reflection?

However you answer these questions, I would like to invite you to consider the following statement: *'Time is our only currency.'* It is the only thing we have until we part from this world. We are so used to our time being sapped by what we tell ourselves that we tend to feel totally out of control with our time. In fact, we tell ourselves we have no choice in how we spend our time. This is a major obstacle facing us in modern life. In fact, we need to go back to basics and find the time to reflect on what emotional pain we avoid.

I hear comments like, 'if only I had more time,' 'I'm so busy – it's difficult to find the time,' or, 'I have too many commitments to spend my time thinking about this.'

When I explain that time is our only currency, people start really thinking about the concept of time. What we choose to do with our time is down to us. So, we use 'I have no time' to avoid some uncomfortable truths about who we are. From my own experiences in cricket I was happy to spend my time doing things that I thought would bring me closer to my dreams. In reality I wasted time on things that were not going to give me that extra yard. Consequently, we learn to avoid things in life because they fill us with fear, anxiety and insecurity to focus our mind on what is really happening. They make us feel vulnerable. So, when we choose to have our coin land on the avoidance side, we begin the process of neglecting ourselves. This is a form of self-harm. We are easily distracted. We find excuses regarding what we do. We ignore others and the uncomfortable truth. We are inflexible, rigid and show no self-care. By not processing what we avoid, we deny ourselves clarity, freedom and joy.

So, does a Special Place automatically come to mind? In your Special Place you will not be rushed, time will stand still as you get immersed in doing something you love just for the pure pleasure of it. Here you are invited not to directly try and answer the avoidance question. Instead, it will be in the back of your thoughts as you engage in doing something fun. For example, you may be painting your favourite wildlife scene or running in the mountains. Here you are relaxed and in an appreciative mode. You are happy because you are doing something you love and you are free from the judgement by self or others. Under these circumstances, you will be stirred perfectly by the avoidance question and as a result, you will start to open up and reflect. Here you will begin to examine your first thoughts and start the process of self-care.

Do you have any idea what they will be?

You will become your very own avoidance mindfulness coach. That is, someone who wants to look in the mirror and consider the experiential avoidance and emotional pain in their life. We are all capable of doing this, but it requires a deep sense of openness and flexibility. You will need to cherish time just to value things in your life for no immediate apparent gain – like looking out at your garden. This avoidance mindfulness will allow you to bring to the surface emotional pain that you hide away from yourself. When your emotional pain appears this is a chance to become aware of it, believe it and self-correct it so that you can reduce its potential impact on your mind, body and soul. You must seize it straight away in order to treat the psychological harm your ego generates. You will need to find and spend time in your Special Place in order to reveal what you avoid in life.

Are you prepared to do this?

Is it difficult to find your Special Place? Are you prepared to slow down and take the time to do nothing? If you are, you will start to see things in your life from a different perspective as what you avoid starts to appear. You will begin to feel uncomfortable and vulnerable as your avoidance and weaknesses that you have been ignoring rise to the surface.

ABC Plan – Stop, look and listen to what you avoid

Finding your special place

So, by working through your own Awareness, Belief and Correction (ABC) Plan you will be in a better position to see how avoidance impacts your life.

Awareness (A): Avoidance Attitude

You will need to examine your attitude towards avoidance in life. Do you agree or disagree that you avoid things while you hunt winning at something? How aware are you of avoidance in life? If you are unaware of what you avoid, you will most definitely be operating with self-importance or selfishly.

Belief (B): Avoidance Behaviour

You will need to assess your avoidance behaviour. Do you ignore your frustrations or conflict with significant people while you are doing something important? Are you able to accept your avoidance behaviour in life? If you ignore how you behave, you are almost certainly functioning with self-importance or selfishly.

Correction (C): Avoidance Values and Beliefs

You will need to consider what your underlying values and beliefs are about things you dream about and fear in life. You will need to consider how you can align your attitudes, behaviours, values and beliefs in order to embrace what you avoid in life. If you choose to cultivate an ABC Personal Change Plan you will actively seek to understand avoidance in your life. This is an essential self-correction needed to shift your values and beliefs towards winning for the benefit of others. The aim of this process is to shift from a winning for oneself (selfish) to winning for others (selfless) perspective. This will give you a deeper level of joy and contentment.

Stop, Look and Listen to What You Avoid

Are you willing and committed to stop, look and listen to your internal traffic regarding what you avoid in your pursuit of winning in your life?

If yes, it requires deep reflection and thinking about what thoughts and feelings are invoked when you pursue winning in life? You will become much more open with yourself. You are capable of doing this, but it requires you to want personal change. It needs you to find a 'Special Place' to stop and think. In my experience, we all have different definitions that constitute a Special Place. For example, for a professional golfer playing in the British Open Championship, his Special Place was a specific song. For one international cricketer playing Test cricket, it is walking along his local beach with his dog. For a Premier League footballer, it is playing music at home on his decks. For a business executive it is going out for long rides on his road bike. For a student, it is returning to the family home for some good old home-cooked food. For a mum, it is going to her yoga class. For the pupil, it is playing with her siblings in her garden. Today, I love nothing more than going to the beautiful surroundings of Stoke Park either to play golf, relax there with my family or to train hard in their gym and take time for personal reflection. To me, this place is like heaven on earth. In your chosen Special Place you can relax and become immersed in doing something joyful in order for the avoidance question to stir your thoughts. Regardless of whether it is a song, person, place or activity, it is about having an opportunity to give yourself time to think about what you tell yourself regarding pursuing winning in life.

What is your Special Place?

Is it difficult to find your Special Place and take time to do nothing?

Are you prepared to do this?

ABC Plan Summary

In Step One, you pressed your own TV remote control on how you go about winning in life; what did the data reveal? In Step Two, you began the process of appreciating your errors; what did your errors tell you? In Step Three, you will take time to find a Special Place to explore what you avoid in life. But take a moment to think about these questions:

- *What are your Special Places in your life? Please list them now.*
- *What is your order of preference from the most favourite to the least favourite?*
- *What is your favourite Special Place and why?*

Can you discuss your answers with someone else, and gain their perspective?

Step Three: Special Place

- *Is winning everything to you?*
- *What have you learnt from Step One?*
- *Do you hate losing?*
- *What have you learnt from Step Two?*
- *What do you avoid when you are trying to beat others?*
- *Do you think beating others is selfish?*
- *What worries you most about losing at something?*
- *What do you avoid when you win?*
- *What do you avoid when you lose?*
- *What conflict do you avoid when you are winning or losing?*
- *What are your frustrations?*

Regardless of whether you are playing sport or in business or education or at home with your family, chasing winning increases the likelihood that you will become selfish. Such selfishness blinds us to what we avoid in life, whether it be internal conflict with self or external conflict with others. Here you desire winning and avoid losing at all costs. Our ego takes over, especially when the pressure is on. What is your reaction under pressure? What do you tell yourself? This is your ego operating. In our Special Place we must learn to see the impact the dark side of winning has on us. Do you become more selfish as you strive to win something? In your Special Place consider your thoughts regarding the following questions:

- What was your initial response or reaction to being in your Special Place and asking yourself such questions?
- Did you resist them or openly try to seek answers?
- Do you feel confident when you win?
- Do you lack confidence when you lose?
- Does it feel uncomfortable to focus on your avoidance about winning and losing in life?
- What do you most become aware of?
- What do you feel – is it enjoyable or does it trigger discomfort?
- What are your uncomfortable truths about the way you win and lose in life? What is the 'elephant in the room' for you?
- What emotions do you choose when you win and lose in life?
- Are you able to see the kind of things you avoid?
- What did you discover about your ego by being in your Special Place?
- Did you enjoy/dislike taking time to stop, look and listen to what you avoid in life?

Time Mindfulness

*Imagine a world where time not money was the only currency. Here the only thing people were interested in and measured you on were how you spent your time and whether it was being productively used for others. Over this **third step**, gaining greater control over how you spend your time is your focus. Here taking time to assess what you avoid in life is vital. Try to assess how* *you spend your time in life by answering the following questions:*

1. *What do you spend your time doing and why?*
2. *What time do you take to consider your attitude and behaviours and their impact on others?*
3. *What time do you take to consider what you avoid?*
4. *Do you give your time freely to others?*
5. *Do you feel you never have enough time and how can you capture back time in your life?*
6. *Do you get sufficient time for yourself?*
7. *Do others criticise you because you give them too little of your time?*

So, which way does your coin end up? Do you focus on not having the time for things, such as reflection? Or do you take time for things that are important to you in life? Of course we all like to think we have all the time in the world. However, we all know we have limited time on this planet. I have discovered that thinking about the precious nature of time is key to gaining more time control and in so doing inspiring others to do the same. I have many experiences of helping others capture more time in order to improve many elements of their life. In so doing it creates momentum for others to do the same. Their positive use of time reduces fear as they are urged to unravel what they avoid. This transforms their thinking and helps others get the most from their time. Re-capturing time is something the best in the world do intuitively. You must groove the appreciation of your time in order to fulfil your potential and operate more selflessly. Having no time puts us into a selfish mode and leads to long-term negative health consequences.

Please select which statement best reflects you when you are about to do something important in life: '*I can't accept losing like that,*' or, '*I'm happy to examine what I avoid.*'

Choice 1. 'I can't accept losing like that'

Avoidance mind-set: Focusing on avoidance is ego (self-importance) driven. You become rigid and inflexible. You are not prepared to spend any time in self-reflection mode. You are dissatisfied. Here you continue to do what you have always done. You refuse to change. You become totally comfortable with what you tell yourself and ignore any information that is telling you something different. Your avoidance of the uncomfortable truth makes you feel much better in the short term. In fact, an episode of avoidance simply leads to other episodes of avoidance. You feel stressed and that something is missing but you ignore what it is. You can potentially experience burnout and fatigue as holding everything in starts to overwhelm you and your avoidance mind-set takes its toll on you. Quality performances are inconsistent. You are inauthentic and lack integrity. Your self-regard is low as a result of avoidance and having no time for reflection prevents you from being happy.

Choice 2. 'I am happy to examine what I avoid'

Non-avoidance mind-set: Having a non-avoidance mind-set is without ego driven. You are open to explore what you avoid in both your performance and life. You understand that looking at the uncomfortable truths in your life is the most effective way of developing who you are. You start to appreciate that your avoidance is not helpful for your team or community. You have a greater vision for your team or community that means that avoidance is unhelpful. You are eager to learn from what you avoid. In fact, you get great pleasure out of learning from what you avoid. You appreciate the benefit to others by taking a non-avoidance attitude to life. You smile at your avoidance and you learn to accept it as an initial reaction to fear in your life. The way you handle avoidance inspires others to take the same journey. They also begin to understand the benefits of not avoiding things in life. You challenge others on things that they avoid and they are encouraged by it and make changes in their life. Avoidance is natural but your ability to embrace it enhances your life and happiness.

Conclusion

This new form of proactive avoidance mindfulness is the start of self-assessment at a much deeper level. By looking at what you avoid when trying to cross the line and win, you will have a window into what your fears are when under pressure. You will see the negative impact on what you tell yourself (ego). It will enable you to see your tension and anxiety when you want to achieve something important. Can you stop, look and listen to avoidance in your life? How committed are you to changing some of your emotional choices under pressure? Does the pursuit of winning feel like you are in a war or does it feel like you are on a beach holiday?

In my experience, this is the most important thing you can do to start the process of understanding what you tell yourself (ego). It is not easy and not for the faint-hearted, but is very rewarding if you are committed to seeing your ego through a new lens.

For example, is winning everything to you? Are you similar to the golfer who refused to consider what he told himself about individual and team events? Or the cricketer who denied what he was feeling on return to international cricket? Or what about the executives who were blinded by their poor relationships?

What potential resistance do you have about avoidance in your life? What comes to mind – the good, the bad and the ugly? This is a difficult process that most people find hard and awkward to do. I have found that people immediately say 'yes, that sounds good' and in principle want to find out about their avoidance but don't have a method of doing it. Unfortunately, however, in a lot of cases people are unwilling to take the time to become more open and discover their personal truth. Hopefully your data from Steps One and Two will allow you to explore what you avoid in this step. We are simply not used to stopping and contemplating what we tell ourselves or accessing our ego.

PART SIX

Outer Ego Programme

(What You Tell Yourself – Seen by Others)

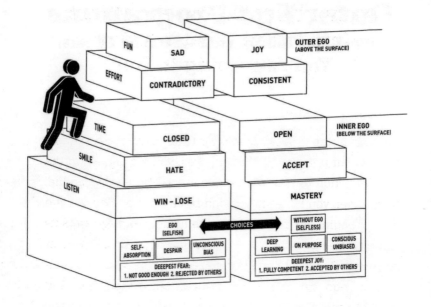

Leadership withoutEGO® Model

20

STEP FOUR: Do You Put Effort into Doing What You Say You Are Going to Do?

• • •

The fourth step to detox your ego is to answer the above question. If your immediate answer is yes, you are headed in the right direction to being free of your ego and happier in life. If, however, you honestly respond by saying no, then you are open to beginning the process of seeing how your ego impacts your life. Being open to your immediate reaction to whether you do what you say you are going to do is key to understanding your ego response. Being inconsistent is dangerous and must change. This is the fourth step to seeing who you really are and how you can truly benefit from winning for others.

'Effort' is the fourth characteristic of ego and it shows you that a separation between what you feel and what you say leads to unhappiness life. By reading through this step you will see how your reaction or response to being consistent indicates whether you detach your feelings from what you say and do. This needs constant checking and changing. You will see how your inconsistency is a selfish act in life. You will see how inconsistency is an ego response. You need to develop a softness towards inconsistency so that you can understand it and self-correct. Building resilience in your life by being softer towards your inconsistency is a difficult and time-consuming process.

Your journey starts with a coin flip and a choice.

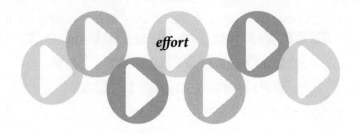

Effort Choice

Whether you know it or not, when you flip your coin of *effort* you have a choice to make. You choose either a 'consistency' or 'say one thing, do another' mind-set. Whichever side your coin lands on will trigger a self-fulfilling prophecy. That is, you will either show inconsistency in your life or you will ensure consistency between your attitudes, behaviour, values and beliefs in your life.

If you choose to be inconsistent in your life, you are choosing an ego reaction. You are choosing to pay attention to fear in your life. This is characterised by the statement: *'I experience separation between what I feel and what I show.'* Clearly, such a reaction means you are in fact inconsistent in how you do things in life. Such separation means you will limit your freedom, happiness and success in life.

However, if you are open to understanding your level of consistency, you are choosing a selfless response as you begin to find a way to be even more helpful to your community. You are choosing to pay attention to joy in your life. This takes courage and is characterised by the statement: *'I do what I say and mean.'*

By definition, elite athletes who cross the line and become world champions are, at this defining moment, at one with how they feel and what they show others. Here they are free, happy and ready for success in life.

 34. STOP: LOOK: LISTEN

Do you deliver what you say and feel?

Are you willing and committed to stop, look and listen to your internal traffic regarding how consistent you are while in pursuit of winning in your life?

If you are, you will need to mind the gap between what you say and what you do in your life.

A Personal Experience of Inconsistency

I grew up watching all kinds of sport – transfixed by the sheer skill of the performer, especially under those pressurised final moments. I was fascinated by how they managed to maintain their consistency under the most extreme conditions. As my need to win and sporting acumen grew, my opportunities to play sport at a high level increased. With mixed feelings of excitement and anxiety, I prepared to play in the biggest football match of my life – I was in the Oxford United Youth Academy team to play Chelsea at Stamford Bridge in the Youth FA Cup. Sitting on the coach as we entered the ground,

I was in awe of the fact that I was about to play on a pitch where my footballing heroes played. As we collected our kit I looked around, amazed by the size and space of the dressing room as well as the carpeted floors.

We excitable young footballers enjoyed the classy and stylish Stamford Bridge stadium; in comparison to our own Manor Ground in Oxford, it was such a departure from what we were used to that we felt like real professionals for the day. As we ran out onto the pitch for the game, it all became a blur as I not only suffered a humiliating performance but we lost 5–0 in the glare of the biggest crowd I had experienced. They were a top team and were so consistent across the park. Many of their players went on to become top players in professional football. I wondered what had stopped me playing as consistently well as I had at other memorable grounds such as the Dell or Vicarage Road. I spent six years playing football at Oxford United and I was always striving to be consistent and get noticed. One training session with the first team I tried to show that I had good enough skills; it was great to show my trickery and love of football in such sessions, but, after, I was struck by the fact that I couldn't produce these skills consistently well enough to become a professional footballer. It was both disappointing and frustrating. The recurring question was why could I perform one day but not the next? What was stopping me being consistent in all I did?

Once again my work with performers in the early days of my psychology career focused on this element. What could I do to help others develop better consistency in their sport than I was able to do in mine all those years ago? I was passionate and hungry to support others to ensure a high level of consistency so that they could learn from my experiences. In cricket, I consulted with a group of players at a second eleven match. After the game I had a discussion with the team regarding the choices they made. This created a stir as I suggested that inconsistent performance was their choice. Some players looked shocked and said nothing while others were keen to comment back. This got a discussion going on the elements of consistent performance that gave me the opportunity to see which players were open and which players were closed. I then suggested that being closed to have an opinion would result in inconsistency on the field of play. Once again this caused much debate and discussion.

One player became really angry at the mere thought that they were choosing their poor performance. This gave me the opportunity to highlight my own failings in cricket as a result of being closed. I then cited examples of world champions that I'd worked with and how they learnt to minimise their ego or selfishness in what they did. More discussion arose, where one player in particular argued back a lot and expressed his feelings about situations out of his control and wanted to know why I was saying it was OK. He asked about poor umpiring decisions, about poor pitches, or about being out of contract. I responded by saying, 'Whatever situation you are in – it is all of your making, it's your choice.'

He was furious and looked at me with utter disdain. My responses were: to counter poor umpiring decisions, I say *'Don't let the ball hit your pads,'* for the poor pitches, I suggested, *'It's about really watching the ball hard and accepting the conditions are the same for everyone,'* for being out of contract, *'Well, you need to play better and become exceptional so that you have contract choices.'* We debated issues quite heavily and intensely. This particular player was out of form, playing in second eleven cricket – a feeling I knew well, so I could really empathise with him. He started to expand on where he was and the fact that his contract was due to expire by the end of the year and he hadn't been offered an extension to date. He was clearly tired, frustrated and angry and my session was only adding to his vexation.

However, there was a turning point in the discussion when I outlined the fact that the world champions I'd worked with learnt to recognise and accept that they are out of control at the moment of crossing the line. He wanted to know more, saying, 'I thought it was all about controlling what you can.' 'No,' I responded. 'It's about developing an acute awareness of when you are out of control and understanding what that situation demands from you in emotional terms.' He started to really listen to what I was saying: 'Take your situation; you're not performing well, not getting selected and, according to you, you are playing with poor umpires and poor batting conditions. What do you do; try harder and refuse to assess what your emotions are telling you? You feel one thing and do the exact opposite – would you say this is true?' 'Yes,' he responded.

'What you should be doing is paying attention to the emotions you are burying at this moment. Do you know what they are and what they represent?' When he replied in the negative, I went on: 'You should be softer and more open to your emotions and respond to what they are telling you. You should close the gap between what you feel and what you are showing us today. This is a chance to bring your feelings together with your actions. What do you say?' After some hesitation he agreed and the discussion continued. Ten minutes or so later, he then began to unravel what he was feeling and what fears he had.

It was a defining moment where the team also started to join in and express themselves in emotional terms. Most of the discussion for the next couple of hours was not about cricket-specific topics but wider concerns. It revolved around how they were feeling both individually and collectively. There was lots of outpouring of emotion. This was like releasing a valve on a pressure cooker. You could see a greater freedom amongst the players, especially this particular one. It was as if the clouds had parted and a beam of sunlight came streaming through as he acknowledged how he was feeling 'below the surface' with his results and actions 'above the surface'. He began to reconcile the differences between them. He accepted that this could be his last year in the game. He accepted that he should let the ball hit his pads. He also accepted and appreciated he had more choice than he was suggesting. From that point on he returned to form, scoring nine hundreds across the rest of the season and winning a new contract for the following year. In conclusion, the team learnt that being totally out of control provides an opportunity to understand how you separate what your emotions are telling you and what you do from day to day. The players began to see this as a privilege situation.

Developing Managers into Transformational Leaders

When a top sales performer does exceptionally well they more often than not get promoted into a managerial role so that they can help others create a sales performance like them.

Sometimes this means their fun stops. As a result, it can be fraught with difficulty as changes in their role may lead to a lack of fun and enjoyment in the new role. On the one hand, they have scored many goals for their business in terms of sales, and it's therefore natural for them to seek promotion. However, on the other hand, such promotion to a management role moves them away from selling; the very thing that gives them joy. It requires a different set of skills.

As a result, they may need extra training and development in order to maximise the opportunity. From my perspective this development is solely around cultivating their awareness of how to have fun through others, when they pass the goal-scoring role to someone else. If they can't do this they are either emotionally trapped in a world of self-absorption and lack emotional intelligence or the role is just not suited to them. Consequently, they may have a more transactional than transformational style. This means they process transactions, say one, two, three – while a transformational person invests their energy in caring for others.

I have seen many top billers, across many industry sectors, gain promotion into a managerial position – only to come up short, not able to adjust their emotional world to cope in the new environment. Such new roles require new levels of emotional understanding as their staff test their leadership skills. We often see this in sport, where a top performer becomes the coach or manager, and then has to manage other top performers. This new role puts him or her into a conflict position as they try to get others performing the way they did. At the heart of this is the need to put effort into learning the new role. A great football example of a player transitioning to a manager is explored below.

This manager played at one of the world's biggest clubs and suggested the past bullying culture in football was not right. When he finished playing he progressed through coaching, scouting and managing, making caring for players central to his leadership style. His style emphasises group culture over the all-about-me culture that can exist in football. Instead, he is focused on serving his community, dedicating his life to genuinely caring for others and reducing fear and anxiety. He ensures that players learn to express themselves freely and with a 'no fear of losing' mind-set. His empathetic style ensures he wins the hearts and minds of everyone involved in the club, especially the players who will always go that extra mile.

 35. STOP: LOOK: LISTEN

What can you contribute to changing the culture of somewhere you work, rest or play in?

Where do you care for others most?

Here the new leader needs to be aware of the different skills required now that they are managing others, as opposed to delivering the results themselves. They need to shift from a *transactional low level* of interaction to a *transformational high-level* interaction, transforming the lives of others. As a result, the new manager begins to show a greater empathy and appreciation of their staff, and finds there is a visible improvement in having fun in their role. A shift to having greater insight and knowledge of winning through others is required. They begin to understand the emotional differences between functioning alone compared to supporting others to achieve more. New managers need to recalibrate their need for recognition in light of helping others succeed by cultivating a desire to see others with their name in lights. This can be a difficult transition.

These new managers will need to accept the change in their work pattern and develop their emotional world so that they are in alignment with the business objectives. This takes a level of emotional maturity and time to learn how to operate without ego. Here a switch of emphasis is required to win through others.

I have seen executives quickly self-correct their level of frustration when their team doesn't follow their lead and do things the way they would do them. This is a great development for new managers who learn that what they did to become successful is not necessarily right for those who report to them; I have seen new managers learn how to curb their anger instead of shouting at staff who don't meet expectations, and many new managers correcting the office culture in the way they deal with difficult situations. This may range from explaining their frustrations to trying to understand the poor performer. They need to challenge their unconscious bias that the individual is simply not good enough or lazy. They need to learn the emotional traps of performance highs and lows from a manager's perspective. They need to learn how to cope with the constant feeling of being judged or threatened by others. They need to learn to find ways of improving underperforming staff.

It is always great to get feedback from staff about their

direct boss. Most of our workplace stress is due to our direct line manager. Therefore getting feedback about their style gives good insight into how satisfying they are to work for. When staff give negative feedback, this is a chance for managers to listen. For example, does the new manager appear nervous or different? The new manager is in transition so may not be as relaxed as he or she once was. This is normal; it is an indication that the new manager needs support on how to understand the notion of serving others.

All too often I see the new manager with an unconscious bias that it is 'all about me', when, in fact, it's always about the team or the organisation. If this is the case there is some work to do. Normally a new manager feels more anxious, and for the first time in his or her career, experiences under-performance. Here there is a contradiction between being a star performer on the one hand, while being a poor performer on the other hand. Work, therefore, becomes immensely stressful for the new manager. The net result is a lower team morale and togetherness leading to poorer levels of sales. The level of collective excellence is reduced and profit is lost. Even though the new manager tries to perform at their best there are unintended consequences for their attitude and behaviour. On the one hand, they perceive they are doing their all to get team performance, while on the other hand, their efforts show signs of simply alienating staff. Clearly getting promotion can lead to misalignment in the business if the win-lose mentality is left unnoticed and untouched.

New managers can face difficulties when transitioning from a functional role to one requiring greater interpersonal skills – managing others. This can create a certain level of discomfort as the once 'top performer' has to learn new ways of taking responsibility for managing staff. In-depth team discussions mean the new manager's style and way of working can be identified. Gathering qualitative data in this way means the team can share their experiences and perceptions of their boss. Here all voices can be heard and understood. This is priceless as a way of accelerating the new manager's ability to win the hearts and minds of their team and take the business forward. In addition, all conflict situations can be explored and clear outputs can be found.

Both new managers and their teams have to accept that building both individual expertise and collective excellence takes time and patience if gains are going to be made. Here a shift from a transactional style to a transformational style is key if the team is to sustain and increase its performance. There needs to be openness and clarity on the values of the new manager, especially when the pressure is on. There needs to be mutual respect and support as well as regular meetings so that members and managers can check in with each other. Discussions over difficult issues, the 'elephant in the room', need to be celebrated. Emotional pain, blockages and unconscious bias need to be understood from a consistency mind-set in order to improve interpersonal relationships. Finally, training on improving transformational leadership is key to developing emotional wellbeing at work. The new manager may explore the following potential interventions to improve the togetherness and performance of their team:

- Increasing their communication and clarifying roles across the team
- Increasing team alignment through better coordination

across all teams, departments and business units

- Designing a transformational leadership programme to help new managers with training and induction into the new role
- Facilitating greater levels of open debate within teams and across departments and gaining 360-degree feedback
- Facilitating succession planning and career development across the organisation
- Eliciting customer feedback to unravel the perception of the company both in terms of products and service delivery and how to develop more specific offerings
- Developing the organisation's incentive and reward programme

Parents

Parents invite me to discuss how I can help improve their child's situation. 'I can't cope with my disruptive child.' In almost all cases, parents have limited awareness of their own contribution to their circumstance, opting to articulate their issue from the perceived 'child problem' perspective – we avoid our own truths in favour of flowing freely with negative feedback for our children. We need to increase our awareness of our own pressing issues before we can handle our own children. In every case, parents are really anxious and worried that their child will not get the best out of themselves and life. They are completely panicked about their child's future, and are eager to ensure their child finds a way of putting the effort in to work harder. They are normally at their wits' end in knowing what to do with their child.

I've found parents avoid being judged by others by

showing an overemphasis on their child's performance at school, their exam results, and attitudes towards teachers and other pupils. The child becomes aware that they are perceived by their parents in a negative fashion, leading them to avoid conversations and feedback about their performance. Both parents and children are frustrated at not being able to communicate this. Further, there are parents who are worried about their child's progress in elite sport. Still others appear anxious about the general motivation of their child, who appears not to be as driven as the parent would like.

Parents are keen to gain a new perspective from talking it through. My general pattern is to meet with the parents and determine their history and context and how they specifically outline their problem. I then usually conduct a meeting with the child to find out their perspective and understand the similarities and differences between them both. Finally, I bring both the parent and child together to seek a new way forward. In each situation, I take time to listen and understand what is happening in both the parents' and child's world. In all cases, both parents and child need the space to consider what is happening. Here avoidance plays a significant role with both the parent and child in their relationship. I would help both the parent and child to see what they were avoiding in their situation.

My ABC Plan Example: An Open Golf Championship Qualifier

The wind was blowing and I was hitting balls on the driving range alongside a professional golfer. In between my play, I was marvelling at his shots being hit to different pins and greens. The sound of the ball strike was crisp and perfect and the swing looked so elegant. We instantly struck up a conversation regarding golf and life in general. This was the start of a long working relationship and friendship that took us from playing golf at our club to me being his caddie on European Tour qualifiers to one of the biggest golf events – the British Open Championship.

It has been a fantastic journey with lots of trials and tribulations along the way. His main dream was to become a world-class golfer. He had represented his club at junior and first team levels. He had also represented the three counties golf at colts and first team levels. He had completed three years of competitive college golf in the United States and was a part of several successful college university teams. He was about to embark on a third competitive year among the professional ranks. As a professional he spent time on tours in Asia, Africa and the UK. This provided lots of opportunities to learn golf in varying conditions and courses. He qualified for a number of professional events over this time. By no doubt, the biggest was qualifying for the British Open. This was one of four major events in the tour calendar. It is every professional's dream to play in a major event. He was so excited and overjoyed at being able to obtain his place for the Open Championship at Turnberry, by securing a par on the eighteenth hole of the International Final Qualifier in Africa. 'I feel a bit shocked and the feeling has not sunk in yet, but I've got mixed emotions and don't know whether to laugh or cry,' he told me.

1. Awareness

My aim was to help him see how he was creating a self-fulfilling prophecy with his inconsistent attitude towards his golf and life. Golf is one of those sports that if you can produce a consistent pattern of scores you will develop your career. As a result, your scores reflect a level of consistency in thinking and feeling. I began to relate his scores to his level of happiness. If he felt no separation between what he was feeling and doing he produced good numbers. However if there was a difference between what he felt and what he shot this was an indication of frustration and sadness. As we began to explore this separation at quite a deep level, he began to see his situation from a very different perspective. We began by discussing the following questions: do you deliver what you say? How do you go about being consistent as a person and as a golfer?

He soon realised that shooting low scores was an indication of how together or separate he was feeling at any one time. If he had issues in his private life then there was trauma on the course. Sometimes this would be a catalyst to play well and sometimes this would destroy his round. We would discuss what was happening and this would allow the potential chance of finding a solution. The notion that everything revolved around his golf was dangerous as he started to separate things out. He began to ruminate over things that were unhelpful and blocked his progress. This would be anything from the Tour officials and other players to the conditions of the course to funding issues. These were all distractions from the stress of having to qualify for Tour events in order to potentially win prize money and in so doing accelerate his progression as a professional player.

It was a tough and difficult process. He was in an extreme position. On the one hand, he had the privilege of pursuing his dream of professional golf – while on the other hand, the pursuit of beating others created internal traffic, rumination and separation in how he truly felt regarding what he was doing. Whilst he loved playing golf, he hated the push to compete with others. This was also reflected in his personal life and being able to hold on to consistently rich relationships. There was competition all round and he was not enjoying it. Over a number of years he became pretty flat and dejected. Qualifying for the Open Championship was the perfect tonic to close the gap between his feeling and actions. At last there was some evidence for his blind faith in his ability as a golfer. As a result, we went about building a plan for the Open Championship. This involved realising who would be the important people in his team and what was needed to be done in the lead up to the Championships.

As a result, we went up to Turnberry in mid-March to look for suitable accommodation, run logistics and walk the course in order to get an initial feel of how to play it. It was an exciting time with lots of banter as thoughts about what was to come filled both our minds. We were both struck by the magnificence of the course and how open and playable it looked. We visited potential homes to rent that were in close proximity to the course. Various decisions were made regarding what accommodation would be best.

2. Belief

Fast forward to late June and the player was preparing to go up again but this time it was for the real thing. He went up early in preparation for the actual Open Championship, starting in mid July. We spoke on the phone and he was shocked at how different the course looked compared to March. Now the rough had grown up and the fairways were looking very narrow indeed. On another call, the player told me how he had lost six balls in his first practice round with the ball only just missing the fairways. I could feel how the pressure of playing in one of the world's biggest events was beginning to impact on him. He needed to increase his level of self-care and provide a cocoon around himself. I was due to fly up to support his preparation the week before it started.

When I arrived at Turnberry, he met me at the entrance to the main pavilion and gave me my accreditation. He looked both excited and nervous all at the same time. He immediately suggested I walk the course while he completed another practice round during the afternoon. As we walked along the course I embraced his brother who was going to be his caddie at this event.

We quickly went to the first hole, where I felt an adrenalin rush as I walked out. It was so different to what I had seen in March. The rough grass had indeed grown out of all proportion and each tee box and fairway had been adorned with banners and roped-off areas to manage the spectators. With the backdrop of the cliffs and sea it represented one of the most picturesque sporting venues I had ever seen. I observed the golfer across all eighteen holes, interested in comparing his play to my knowledge of what I'd seen before. It was fascinating.

Each day of practice rounds was similar; he would sign up to a practice round time slot and play alongside some of the best golfers to ever have played the game. On one round he was fortunate to play alongside two former multiple major championship winners who were icons of the game. It was truly remarkable and an honour to be walking the course with these two greats. For the player it was a dream come true. He simply couldn't believe his luck to be pegging his ball up with these two legends. It was great to hear the banter and watch them relax him and play with such ease. After several days of practice we were in one of the practice areas; here the player was in a bunker hitting balls to various pins when he stopped and turned round to reveal his apprehension about the start of the tournament. A way of self-correcting his anxiety was established.

3. Correction

His anxiety grew as he began to think about what he was approaching the following day. He started to look panicked and nervous about the enormity of the event. His immediate concern was worrying about whether he would be able to compete on such a stage alongside many world-class golfers. It was difficult to keep him relaxed as he paid attention to all the worst that could possibly happen. He was eager to find a solution as he floated balls out of the bunker. In between his shots we discussed finding a way to help him feel better about what he was about to do.

We spoke about many different things relating to his feelings. At this stage he was as open as I could ever remember. He began to speak about some deeply held beliefs and anxieties he had in life. It was clear that the event had invoked a strong emotional reaction I'd never seen before. It was like the dark stormy weather conditions were about to descend on our practice area.

We discussed a number of potential solutions but nothing seemed to calm him. Here he was experiencing some of the worst levels of anxiety whilst also producing a deftness of touch in his bunker play. It was absorbing and fascinating stuff. We carried on talking while he performed some great shots and he started to recall a similar separation between how he felt and what he did. I probed a little deeper and he revealed a story about breaking up with a long-term girl-friend. The story went that whilst on the golf range in South Africa, he was hitting balls and feeling awful. He spoke about his poor ball strike and flight knowing he was about to com-pete in a tournament. He didn't know how he was going to do it when all of a sudden, someone's phone rang and the ring tone triggered an emotional shift in him.

I asked him to tell me more. He went on to describe the importance of this specific song and how it had helped him many times in the past to reconcile his feelings with what was happening in his relationships. You could see the relief start to germinate within as he began to bring his feelings in line with his actions. For whatever reason, he was gaining perspective on what he was doing. He was reducing his sep-aration between how he was feeling and what he was doing.

I asked him about the song and he began to sing the words and the entire atmosphere improved. I suggested it would be great to get to the range and hit some balls while he had chosen to shift his internal weather conditions to a bright sunny day. We proceeded to the range where he produced some of the best shots I'd ever seen him hit. He was freer and happier which manifested in great ball strike and flight. We were all taken back by his immediate freedom and quality. He was in his Special Place as he sang the words to a very meaningful song while he hit some great shots with all his clubs. It was a great moment. He had found something to help keep his mind-set from being pulled apart while under extreme pressure. He found a way to protect his confidence from draining away and to hold on to something that would give him some control over his consistency. We finished the practice and went off back to the rented house for some food and family time.

The Defining Moment

The next morning we were ready for the tournament. The weather was fantastic and Turnberry was a magnificent sight. The golfer appeared different. He was relaxed and looked alert and ready for the biggest exposure of his career. His fears about being good enough and negatively judged by others had subsided. He was keen to maintain being in his Special Place.

When on the first tee his name was called, a massive gallery had appeared. This was breaking new ground for him, as he had never played golf under such scrutiny. He looked relaxed and took a four iron for fairway position and struck it beautifully down the middle. Here he was about to experience his defining moment as he birdied the first three holes and was on the leaderboard of this major championship after nine holes. On the tenth green he had another putt for birdie when he heard a fairway reporter mention his name. Unfortunately he got distracted and sent the putt flying past the hole. He not only missed the birdie putt but he also missed the putt coming back. He experienced catastrophic stress as he bogeyed the hole, leading to a few more bogeys.

You could see the frustration visibly etched on his face. He began to gradually separate his feelings of angst with his golf mastery at this point. The gap between the two became significantly bigger as the round progressed and he slid out of contention. Although he couldn't recapture his consistency, he was left with a euphoric feeling of playing in the biggest tournament of his entire life and career – the oldest major championship in the world and one he had dreamt of playing in since he was a small boy.

Today, he is using his passion for golf as one of the co-founders of a new creative golf game that encourages both young and old to take up golf. He has been able to coordinate both world-class golfers and celebrities to raise awareness of this new game whilst also raising significant money for great causes.

Your ABC Plan: Minding the Gap

Ask yourself the following questions: do you hide your feelings away from others? Or is there a difference between what you say and do? Do you find it hard or easy to be consistent at what you do?

If you have answered 'yes' to any of the above questions, you will need to consider the following: when you are doing something important, can you learn to mind the gap between what your inner traffic is saying and what you have to do?

Paying attention to negative thinking from others is very disturbing and very dangerous. For example, imagine you are at a party and you overhear a friend talking badly about you. What do you do? Do you confront them or do you bury how it makes you feel? Again, as with all the other steps, what you decide will become a self-fulfilling prophecy. I'm sure you are fully aware that negativity or hurtful comments expressed by others has the potential to trigger deep rumination within us. You become anxious and tense thinking about the comments made and how you are feeling. At this point, if you decide to ignore your feeling, a gap starts to appear between how you feel and what you do. Such separation is dangerous and needs to be processed.

Over time, the process of burying feelings and emotions and choosing to separate how you feel with how you behave uses lots of energy and leads to stress and ill health. Not expressing yourself on a regular basis to many people or just a few can create a bad habit. Such a habit can deepen your emotional pain. It needs to be addressed. In this step, I want you to become the 'watchman at the gate' over who provides you with interaction that is negative and dark and who provides interaction that is positive and light. Can you immediately think of people who sit in these two camps in your life? How does it make you feel looking at this list?

The aim is to provide a sanity check on those around you who either blow your tyres up – or let the air out of them. Do you surround yourself with people that uplift you? Or do you choose individuals that bring you down? If you choose the latter, do you let them know the impact they are having on you? Or do you simply ignore your feelings?

Increasing your awareness of how you separate feelings from action impacts your health and happiness. A big gap between them is dangerous and can lead to high levels of stress and ill health. You should work very hard to close the gap between your feelings and action in order to increase your health and happiness. In this step, you will become your very own watchman at the gate so that you can constantly scan and check what your gaps are and who is influencing you in either a positive or negative way.

Now, look at your lists of positive and negative people and

consider this. Do you treat people on those lists differently? If the answer to this is yes then you need to start the process of self-correction. You will need to ask yourself why you treat people differently. There is a paradox emerging. On the one hand, you have produced a list of people that trigger light and dark within you, while on the other hand, you acknowledge that you are inconsistent in how you treat others. You will need to address your own inconsistency for health and happy living.

How do you go about reconciling differences between what you say and what you do? How can you become more consistent with everyone? How can you begin the process of being open with what you feel? These are difficult questions to resolve. Your challenge starts today. In order to self-correct your gap you must be prepared to be open and look at your inconsistencies. Your inconsistencies in how you treat others are there for a reason. There must be some benefit to what you feel, say and do. Do you know what your benefit is?

The process is to be mindful of any separation you have and understand why it exists in order to become more consistent in what you feel and do. It is as if you are finding a way to combine different channels of information, such as watching the TV while listening to the radio. The skill is to actively listen to both independently and then blend them to enrich your experience. Your major battle with inconsistency is to simply know when you are being inconsistent/consistent and the reasons why. The examples in this step will attempt to shed light on how our ego maintains a state of inconsistency that is at best anxiety-provoking and at worst a trigger for prolonged stress and even depression. Being able to deliver and sustain what you say and do is dependent on greater insight about what you tell yourself as a result of the interaction with those around you.

In summary, when you feel the negative judgement of others, it automatically triggers your ego and you will be heightened to criticism and negativity. You may begin to feel bad about yourself, choosing a low degree of freedom with what you do and a low self-regard. Our self-esteem is driven by what others think. Unfortunately, your ego is only trying to help you process the perceived impending threat of being negatively judged by others; it is our natural defence system.

ABC Plan – 'Doing What You Say and Feel'

'Mind the Gap'

So, by working through your own Awareness, Belief and Correction (ABC) Plan you will be in a better position to see if there is a gap between what you say and what you do in life.

Awareness (A): Consistent Attitude

You will need to put effort into examining whether you have a consistent or inconsistent attitude in life. E.g. Do you say one thing but do another? Do you agree or disagree that you are consistent in all you do and say when you hunt winning at something? How aware are you of your level of consistency in life? If you are unaware of being consistent, you will most definitely be operating with self-importance or selfishly.

Belief (B): Consistent Behaviour

You will need to assess if your behaviour is consistent or contradictory. Do you ignore your inconsistency with significant people when you are doing something important? Are you able to accept your inconsistent behaviour in life? If you ignore your inconsistent behaviour, you are almost certainly functioning with self-importance or selfishly.

Correction (C): Consistent Values and Beliefs

You will need to consider how your underlying values and beliefs are about things you dream about and fear in life. You will need to consider how you can align your attitudes, behaviours, values and beliefs in order to embrace your consistency in life. If you choose to cultivate an ABC Plan you will actively seek to close the gap between how you feel and what you do. This is an essential self-correction needed to shift your values and beliefs towards winning for the benefit of others. The aim of this process is to shift from a winning for oneself (selfish) to winning for others (selfless) perspective. This will give you a deeper level of joy and contentment.

Are you willing and committed to stop, look and listen to your internal traffic regarding the difference between what you say and what you do in your pursuit of winning in your life?

If yes, it requires reflection and thinking about what thoughts and feelings are invoked and to separate how you behave in your pursuit of winning in life. You will need to increase your tolerance of ambiguity in order to close the gap between what you say and do. We are all capable of doing this, but it requires an open desire for personal change.

Mind the Gap

For example, one Saturday morning an executive at home was getting overtly angry and shouted at his children who were playing but were teasing each other. He admitted that his reaction was unreasonable and disproportionate and he didn't understand why the situation made him feel so angry. He was unhappy about who he was becoming. He began to unravel his true feelings. You could visibly see him unwinding and starting to release much pent-up emotion. He outlined how, over the last few months, he was under enormous pressure at work. He was being blamed for a business deal not going through although he never spoke out or countered the claim. Instead, he chose to power down and not address those who were accusing him and to get on with stuff and work even harder. In effect, he was acting like a TV in standby mode. That is, he was ready to be put 'on' but he was 'off'. Basically, he felt one thing (frustrated at being accused) but acted the opposite (just ignored his feelings). He disregarded this for months until it presented itself in the form of anger at his children. A number of issues became clear through our discussion. First, he needed to reconcile the gap between his feelings and action, specifically at work. He set meetings up with various people to outline what had happened to the project. Secondly, he needed to close the gap in his attitude and behaviour at home. That is, be able to explain to his family that the children bickering was not the real issue underlying his anger. Finally, he began to realise the importance of processing his true feelings and actions so that he was able to reduce saying one thing but doing another. What he discovered was that unresolved work issues were impacting his family life. By exploring his inconsistent attitude and behaviour at both work and home he was able to see the conflict situation at work from a different perspective. He became more productive and happier at both work and home.

To summarise, I have seen executives put a huge amount of commitment into their work that spills over into their home life. They choose to sacrifice everything in order that their company achieves its ambitions. I have seen executives sacrifice family life in order to complete the business deal or sacrifice their friends while in pursuit of satisfying the hunger of their organisation. Many executives even sacrifice their health in order to feel they are attending to the needs of their bosses by working impossible hours with little sleep and poor diets. Some feel burnout, stressed and empty. Others feel sad, isolated and lonely. When I ask: 'Why are you doing this to yourself? Why are you not caring for yourself better?', there is always an initial puzzled look of frustration and a response of 'I have no choice'. In every case, the executive opens up and highlights their inconsistent and contradictory position.

They are everything at work. Nothing at home. They feel separated by doing one thing to serve the business but doing the opposite thing at home. As the separation between the two gets bigger and bigger they find it almost impossible to reconcile the difference between the two. This is very dangerous and must be immediately addressed. Here the 'mind the gap' activity is used to help reduce the difference between what they feel and what they do. The aim is to significantly align attitude and behaviour in all environments and to generate alignment between work and home. This always leads to a debate about choice, time and how they are used.

Helping people to face the question of being consistent in life always creates slight anxiety and discomfort. When you explore differences between what is said and done it is stressful. I have had many discussions with senior executives about how consistent they are in life. Some find explaining their differences easy while others get agitated by their inconsistency. They want to make change happen immediately. Such individuals understand that their ability to influence those around them significantly increases if they are seen as a consistent, happier person. Being able to genuinely inspire others depends on whether you are consistent in what you do. Inconsistent people lose credibility and their personal brand is not taken seriously. You must choose to close the gap on your inconsistencies.

I believe that executives who are consistent show a higher degree of selflessness at work. Whereas executives who are inconsistent have a higher degree of selfishness. Discussion over the merits of selfishness and selflessness in business is always intriguing. Helping individuals understand how to use their leadership gifts through being more consistent is great fun and always challenging.

ABC Plan Summary

First I would like to summarise where we are up to regarding the activities you have performed. In Step One, you have pressed your own TV remote control on how you go about winning in life; what did the data reveal? In Step Two, you began the process of appreciating your errors; what did you errors tell you? In Step Three, you took time to find a Special Place to explore what you avoid in life; what did taking the time to do this reveal? Now, in Step Four, you will be asked to examine the difference between what you feel and what you do by responding to the following questions:

- *Is it difficult to cope with the conflict between what you feel and how you perform?*
- *Is it hard to tolerate the difference between your feelings and actions?*
- *How do you cope with contradiction in life?*
- *How do you reconcile the differences between your feelings and actions?*
- *What feelings and actions do you separate in life?*
- *Do you feel frustration with inconsistent performance?*

- *Do you think that feeling one thing and doing another thing is a selfish act?*

Step Four: Mind the Gap

In your 'mind the gap' activity, you might want to consider your thoughts regarding the following questions:

- *Is winning everything to you?*
- *What have you learnt from Step One?*
- *Do you hate losing?*
- *What have you learnt from Step Two?*
- *What do you avoid when you are trying to beat others?*
- *Do you think beating others is selfish?*
- *What worries you most about losing at something?*
- *What do you avoid when you win?*
- *What do you avoid when you lose?*
- *What conflict do you avoid when you are winning or losing?*
- *What are your frustrations?*

Regardless of whether you are playing sport or in business or education or at home with your family, chasing winning increases the likelihood that you will become selfish. Such selfishness increases our inconsistency in life, for example by feeling one thing but doing another thing. Here your desire is to manage the separation between your feelings and actions. Our ego takes over, especially when the pressure is on. What is your reaction under pressure? What do you tell yourself? This is your ego operating. In minding the gap you must learn to see the impact the dark side of winning has on us. Do you become more selfish as you strive to win something? In minding the gap, consider your thoughts regarding the following questions:

- What was your initial response or reaction to differences between what you feel and what you do?
- Do you ignore or hide feelings from yourself?
- Do you act in ways you sometimes regret? If so, what are they?
- How do you go about reconciling differences between your attitude and behaviour?
- Did you resist reconciling the differences between your feelings and actions or openly try to seek to ensure they get aligned?
- Does it feel uncomfortable to focus on your inconsistencies and contradictions about winning and losing in life?
- What do your inconsistencies tell you?
- How do you tolerate your inconsistencies and contradictions?
- What emotions do you choose when you are being inconsistent with others in life?
- Are you able to see the kind of things you avoid?
- What did you discover about your ego by addressing your inconsistencies?

Effort Mindfulness
Imagine a world where as soon as you experienced any inconsistency or contradiction between what you feel

and what do you it gets immediately resolved. How happy would you be? Others immediately see your authenticity and integrity as you quickly align feelings and actions in your life. Over this **fourth step***, try to gain greater control by adjusting and monitoring your dials for your feelings and actions, like you are changing the settings between your treble button and bass button on your music system in order to enjoy the perfect sound. Here, assessing and correcting the differences between attitudes and behaviours gives your life meaning and joy. Try to assess and monitor differences between your attitude button and your behaviour button by answering the following questions:*

1. *What is the first thing you notice about the differences and similarities between your attitude and behaviour, especially when you are trying to win at something?*
2. *What conflicts, contradictions and inconsistencies exist between your attitudes and behaviour as you attempt to win at something?*
3. *How do you go about aligning your differences between what you feel and what you do?*
4. *Are others aware of your internal inconsistencies?*
5. *Do you feel vulnerable as if they could see what's inside your head?*
6. *What methods do you use to resolve differences between your feelings and actions?*
7. *How quickly can you reconcile differences between your attitudes and behaviours?*

So, which way does your coin end up? Do you focus on managing the gap between what you say and do? Or do you look to ensure you experience a oneness between your attitudes and behaviour? Of course you would like to be consistent in all you do in life. However, you know that at times this is not possible. I have discovered that aligning the gap or separation between attitudes and behaviour is vital to increase health and happiness. I have many experiences of helping others reconcile their differences in feelings and actions in order to improve many elements of their life. In so doing it creates momentum for others to do the same. Their positive alignment between attitudes, behaviours, values and beliefs reduces fear as they feel they have become a more complete person. This transformation inspires others to do the same and get the most from their life. Realigning attitude and behaviour is something the best in the world do intuitively. Having no misalignment puts us into a selfish mode and leads to long-term negative health consequences.

Please select which statement best reflects you when you are about to do something important in life: '*I am so frustrated by my inconsistent performance*,' or, '*I constantly strive for consistency in how I feel and what I say and do.*'

Choice 1. 'I am so frustrated by my inconsistent performance'

Inconsistent mind-set: Being inconsistent is ego (self-importance) driven. You ignore the difference between what you feel, say and do. You are not tolerant of ambiguity but find a way to live with all your contradictions. You ignore the tension of feeling one thing but doing another and plough on. Here you continue to achieve inconsistent results. Some days are good while other days are bad. You find it difficult to resolve your inconsistent results and the way you feel. In the end, your ego-driven mind-set enables you to find an adequate explanation for your inconsistency in life whether at work or at home. You spend significant time just holding feelings in and managing your impression with others. You lack authenticity and at times people question your integrity. You see this but choose to ignore it. You feel frustrated that others don't see the true you. The energy expended may lead to burnout and fatigue as managing the difference between what you say and do impacts every part of your life. You feel separation between what is going on inside with what is happening on the outside. Your self-regard is low, as inconsistencies in your life are not processed at a deep enough level to make change happen.

Choice 2. 'I constantly strive for consistency in how I feel and what I say and do'

Consistent mind-set: Having a consistent mind-set is without ego driven. You are open to explore the difference between what you say and what you do. You are able to tolerate the ambiguity that comes with being inconsistent and you work hard to resolve it. You realise that inconsistent attitudes and behaviours are not acceptable and you are happy and put effort into making change happen by reconciling your differences. You begin to ask yourself what both consistency and inconsistency look like in your life. You begin to see that consistency is a powerful agent of influence on others, either your team or community. Your vision and purpose result in you continuously resolving your inconsistency. You get great pleasure out of learning from your inconsistency by self-reflection and getting feedback from significant others. You smile at your inconsistency and you learn to understand the gap between what you say and do. You accept the gap is an initial reaction to fear in your life. The way you handle inconsistency inspires others to take the same journey. They also begin to understand the benefits of being more consistent in life. You challenge others on their inconsistency and they are encouraged by it and make changes in their lives. You learn that being inconsistent is a natural by-product in life but your ability to embrace it enhances your life and happiness.

Conclusion

This consistency-inconsistency mindfulness allows you to explore your feelings, thoughts and actions in a much deeper way. By looking at your level of consistency when trying to cross the line and win, you will begin to develop a window into what your fears are when under pressure. You will see the negative impact on what you tell yourself (ego). It will enable you to see your inconsistency when you want to achieve something important. Can you stop, look and listen to your level of consistency your life? How much effort and commitment are you prepared to put in to close the gap between what you say and do when you are under pressure? How do you resolve being inconsistent in front of others? Does the pursuit of winning feel like you are in a war or does it feel like you are on a beach holiday?

21

STEP FIVE: Do You Have Fun?

. . .

The fifth step to detox your ego is to answer the above question. If your immediate answer is yes to this question, you are headed in the right direction to being free of your ego and happier in life. If, however, you honestly respond by saying no, then you are open to beginning the process of seeing how your ego impacts your life. Being miserable is dangerous and must change. 'Fun' is the fifth characteristic of ego and it shows you how experiencing joy in life enhances your emotional freedom. You will see how not having fun is a selfish act in life.

This is the fifth step to seeing who you really are and how you can truly benefit from winning for others. By reading through this step you will see how your reaction or response to having fun indicates your selfishness or selflessness in your life. You will see how not having fun is an ego response. You need to develop a softness towards not having fun so that you can understand it and self-correct. Building resilience in your life by being softer towards your lack of fun is a difficult and time-consuming process.

Your journey starts with a coin flip and a choice.

fun

Fun Choice

Whether you know it or not, when you flip your coin of *fun* you have a choice to make. You choose either to 'have fun, or 'feel miserable'. Whichever side your coin lands on will trigger a self-fulfilling prophecy. That is, you will either show joy in whatever you do or appear unhappy with whatever you do.

If you choose to not have fun in your life, you are choosing an ego reaction. You are choosing to pay attention to fear in your life. This is characterised by the statement: *'I am sad and emotionless when I'm performing.'* Clearly, such a reaction means you are not having fun with what you do in life. Such sadness means you will limit your freedom, happiness and success. However, if you are open to having fun in life, you are choosing a selfless response as you begin to find a way to be even more helpful to your community. You are choosing to pay attention to joy in your life. This takes courage and is characterised by the statement: *'I see the humour in difficult situations.'*

By definition, elite athletes who cross the line and become world champions are, at this defining moment, completely happy with who they are and what they are doing. Here, they are free, happy and ready for success in life.

36. STOP: LOOK: LISTEN

Do you have fun?

Or are you willing and committed to stop, look and listen to your internal traffic regarding how much fun you are having whilst in pursuit of winning in your life?

If you are, you will need to learn to make every day like a Saturday in your life.

A Personal Experience of Joy

During my cricket career, I decided to spend two winter seasons in Australia in an attempt to significantly improve my skills and performance. I left the UK to take up a role as the captain and coach of a small rural cricket club, in the outskirts of the Melbourne area.

It was here I discovered something new about myself. Firstly, I realised I needed to be happy with what I was doing in life and have support. I was on the other side of the world, literally, doing something I loved while away from my family, with the support of my girlfriend (who would in time become my wife and mother to our four beautiful children). Back home in England, I had the support of not only my family but also my girlfriend's family. In addition, importantly, I had the support of the president of the club who had a vision of improving the fortunes of this local club. He also believed in my vision.

Secondly, I was appointed club captain and coach, responsible for sharing my vision for the game over this two-year period, while helping to nurture the club's next generation of young players. It was great to influence the club both on and off the field as well as share stories from my professional cricket experience.

Finally, I had a chance to experience the fun of Australian culture and the ability to share it with someone special to me. I had the best of both worlds; it felt like every day was a Saturday. It was brilliant all round. Our relationship flourished and the club had one of its most successful periods in its history. I had high levels of parity, control and personal meaning – all vital ingredients to being happy.

Australia had proven the breeding ground for being happy in life. We had a great time and were looked after incredibly well. Not surprisingly this warm feeling inside had a significant impact on my performances and I began to shine and play consistently well. I bowled with pace and enthusiasm, taking regular wickets and helping our side to success. I became a consistent performer and felt contentment and happiness at being able to execute my skills consistently and successfully under pressure. As a person I began to grow and feel a strong sense of high self-regard. In addition I continued my master's degree in psychology, keen to understand my performance, my life and myself.

When I returned home to the UK for my county, my performances became much more consistent. In practice matches against first class opposition, I bowled fast with greater control and took wickets. I began to feel that I would have the impact in the game that I yearned for. Unfortunately, the manager who brought me in got sacked. However, with my newfound consistency, I started to bowl really well and began to take lots of wickets in the second team. This helped lessen the impact of my mentor no longer being at the club. I naively thought that if I continued to produce these good performances I would secure a place in the first team. However, after a number of these good performances I was still not getting selected so I decided to call a meeting with my second team coach, the county manager and the first team captain to try and understand what was behind my lack of selection. After several minutes it became clear that they thought I was playing well but regardless of my performances, they informed me that I wasn't in their planning for the future and so I was not going to be selected for first team cricket. Strangely I felt overjoyed at hearing this news as I was beginning to feel frustrated at my lack of selection. I now had clarity that my selection was not based solely on performance. I felt free as I had developed a certain level of competence in my play. I then asked if I could resign and leave the club instantly, which they agreed. Consequently, I left half way through my second year and I felt a real sense of freedom.

I had retired from the professional game at the age of twenty-six. However, I no longer felt the same sense of disappointment as I had at my first county; I was happy that I'd developed a level of competence in my game. I was able to accept the emotional rollercoaster of professional sport and I felt happy I had given it my all. I also felt free to retire and, although I hadn't played as much first class cricket as I would have liked, I was satisfied with the outcome. I had played with some of the best cricketers in the world and some of my cricketing heroes at two of the biggest clubs in the country.

I had literally travelled the world and experienced new cultures, new things and had fallen in love. I was happy to take the next chapter of my life but continued to focus on developing a value-based way of living.

I was able to concentrate on completing my master's degree in occupational psychology, with the added benefit that my girlfriend no longer needed to commute to the Midlands each weekend, meaning we could build on the relationship that had developed so strongly in Australia. Although I was no longer pursuing my dream of first class cricket, I was now free to pursue my other passion – psychology. Life felt great and I was eager to make the transition into my new career.

I was able to combine both my love for cricket with my passion for psychology working for the England and Wales Cricket Board as a county development officer, a role I was to work in for the next five years. I created a structure for more young people to play through the development of district cricket. The aim of district was to give opportunities to young people to play cricket just below county level; in doing so, it was hoped that the 'gap' between school/club cricket and county cricket would be reduced. Other benefits of the district process included increasing the number of players involved with quality cricket, and attracting young people who may never have played cricket before, but who had the natural ability to learn and progress to the top.

I was appointed to chair one of the ECB's working groups, designing an ECB Development Pathway. Here I was responsible for creating a new infrastructure for developing young people, in line with the ECB Performance Plan, aiming to create the right motivational climate for young people to develop in cricket. I also developed a psychology educational programme for all county cricketers. My county saw the benefits of a four-year development programme, which built in performance criteria to monitor programme effectiveness. I also became an ECB Level III Coach during this time, becoming responsible for providing advanced training to the best coaches in the county.

My ABC Plan Example: A Premier League Academy and the Use of Psychology

I had the fantastic opportunity of being invited to present my ideas at one of the biggest Premier League clubs in the world. I was so excited when I arrived at the training ground and gave my name at the security gate. It was such a thrill to see all the perfect manicured football pitches alongside various indoor training centres. The sheer space to play and have fun was incredible, a real contrast to my experience of training back in a local park in Oxford. It was an unbelievable environment for playing football.

When I arrived I was met by one of the physiotherapists, who showed me around the facility. It was a great insight into the extent of professionalism at the highest level of the game, where nothing was left to chance, from the right food and the way it was cooked, to the medical and sport science support, even down to how the buildings were cleaned. There was an air of quality about what everyone in the club did, regardless of what role the person covered; this came from the inspirational manager who expected high standards, whether you were the cook, the cleaner, the first team coach or player. The intensity about the place was clear to see. There was a taken-for-granted attitude of knowing how to execute a performance.

It was amazing to see the detail the club went into. Visiting the world-class gym and strength and conditioning room, I watched players stand in front of an arched screen, reacting to various light displays by pushing the relevant buttons; this was gathering data on each player's visual acuity. The club had collected years of data on players so that they knew which players, in which positions, had the best peripheral vision. This was seen as a vital skill for seeing the play early and making the best use of the ball.

I was then taken to a large room for my presentation to the club's coaches. There were about forty coaches in attendance including the academy director, reserve team coaches, youth team coaches and a recently retired international first team player.

Before I explained my perspective on how psychology could help them as coaches, I wanted to explore their thinking about who were the best ever players to play for the club. The coaches were put into small groups and asked individually to list their top five, and to discuss their selection within their group. As I walked round each group, the level of continuity in name selection astounded me; each group had a level of conformity in the names, bar one or two disagreements. As they fed back their agreed list, I started to probe about why there was such uniformity across all groups. This created much discussion and revealed more about how the club was run with its clear history, leadership, the fervour about how football should be played, and what was expected of each and every player that played for the club. The level of alignment, across all areas of the club, was remarkable, from the chairman to the manager through to the coaches and players.

It was interesting to hear from the players' perspective how effective the club was at communicating and translating the necessary knowledge and know-how, so the players understood what decisions they were responsible for every minute of the game. There was a complete shared mind-set regarding their role with young players. This was to ensure they made the right decisions at the right time, especially when faced with the enormity of representing this club. It was obvious from their shared understanding that this was a weighty responsibility.

We discussed the importance of moving away from a win-at-all-costs mentality, to one focused on having fun playing football, especially when it came to younger players. None of the coaches disagreed with it in principle, but asked about how to create that fun environment – especially when there were high expectations that the club win every match. We agreed this was difficult, so I outlined the need to motivate players by the desire to have fun and help them understand how to choose fun as an internal climate instead of a sad internal climate.

I pointed to the importance of relationships as they are so significant in our choice of emotions at any one time; this was especially true when it came to the young, impressionable players. There needed to be a close emphasis on the relationships within the club for each young player, involving all vested parties, from school teachers, welfare officers and parents to coaches, physios and obviously the player himself. There was general agreement that more fun should be engendered, and a spirit of openness, with each young player being allowed to express himself freely. However the need to perform and win was always under the surface.

Some years later I worked closely with a manager who was a former player at the club and who had the same shared values and way of working as these coaches. In a way, it gave me a good head start in getting to know him and supporting his approach alongside his assistant. Here is an outline of an ABC Plan for this manager and his assistant.

My ABC Plan Example: A Football League Manager and his Assistant

1. Awareness

The manager and his assistant were two former Premier League players and were both full of experience and quality. I was asked by the assistant manager to come and have a look at how they were working and give my observations.

Their understanding and love for the game was in no doubt. The manager was a former international player and had captained a host of teams at the highest level, including his country, while his assistant had a long playing career at the highest level and played internationally at under-21's level. As a pure student of the game, studying every aspect of both his team and the opposition, he was a meticulous planner and loved assessing the finest details of the game. He had a deep appreciation of the game both as an effective player, as well as an effective technical coach. He had the ability to be able to see what was required from a playing perspective and effectively communicate what changes an individual or unit needed to do to neutralise the threat from any opposition. Combining his knowledge and know-how with his manager meant that they would discuss at length their team in relation to the opposition and how they were going to set up. Sometimes they would have heated exchanges in order to get to the necessary solutions regarding team selection and style of play. This was a natural part of their process of getting the team ready to perform. Their depth of their relationship meant that they understood each other to the point that there were no misunderstandings or miscommunication; disagreeing with each other was a positive experience. They were just focused on ensuring their decision-making and football mastery were aligned. It was great to see.

They were two experienced players and coaches who loved getting involved with training their players. The banter and jokes were great and the practice was of high quality. They would both get involved and create an environment of high performance with lots of fun. There was lots of noise as both staff and players were free to express themselves. It was a very positive environment and you could see everyone loving it. They were so thorough in their planning, preparation and quality. They would generate a deep sense of purpose through their ability to communicate their knowledge or message to the players. In fact, they were able to translate what they were saying by not only showing their ideas on video analysis but also being able to demonstrate exactly the play they wanted to see delivered by the players. It was all very powerful stuff.

Clearly, my feedback was extremely positive and it was a delight being around them.

However, their mood on match day was completely different. Here you could see their tension and anxiety. They appeared on the edge of their emotions. I saw frustration and anger spill over on the touchline with players and officials alike. I witnessed high levels of rage during the match and, when the team was losing, I saw players quiet, with their heads bowed – totally different to training. It was a complete contrast.

At the next training session, I pointed out the contrasting emotions during training with those during matches to the assistant; he was keen to explain the obvious. 'The fun goes when you need a win, and it's all about getting the result,' he suggested. 'That's the problem with the focus being on the win,' I replied.

2. Belief

The assistant was very open to talking things through. He accepted that he was operating in a very stressful environment, and found it helpful to talk confidentially through some of his frustrations in the game. He outlined some of his difficulties with the individuals across the entire club, including players and executives. As a player he would have loved more opportunity to have someone to talk with as his negative emotions built up into confrontations with others, so he knew that dealing with how he was feeling was important. He had a high level of acceptance that not understanding his emotional world had led to real bother. He was keen not to make the same mistakes in management and wanted to have more fun. He also wanted to improve his personal brand in the game and be seen as a quality technical coach.

3. Correction

Consequently, he soon recognised that his anger was more indicative of his deeply held emotions. We then began to explore what triggered negative emotions in him. Lots of things were discussed and it was clear that his win-at-all-costs attitude was the main contributor. This was not new to him but talking about winning being a selfish act that interfered with the love he had for the game seemed to stop him in his tracks. Being made aware of coaching football from a selfless perspective reduced his level of anger and fear. He immediately recognised the need to serve others more by having fun. He was able to self-correct his feeling to have fun when he was about to derail. He began to get immersed in his methodology of preparing and coaching the team.

The Defining Moment

One of his defining moments came when he had the chance to manage the team in the absence of the manager. You could see him relishing the opportunity; he appreciated his role and position, and ensured he maintained his composure and grace on the touchline through the games in charge. His demeanour was a reflection of his understanding and love of the sport, and his calmness demonstrated his ambassadorial role for the club as a leader. In addition, he was able to translate this into extensive support for his community; I was, and am, proud of the difference he made.

Your ABC Plan: Making Every Day a Saturday

Ask yourself the following questions: do you create a bright, sunny internal climate when you perform? Or is your internal climate dark and stormy?

The key to sustained performance and happiness is to choose a bright sunny internal climate when you are performing. This is not to say you can't perform in darkness, as I'm sure we have all chosen this state at times in our life. The point is that to sustain great decision-making under pressure requires a clear, calm head. For example, what is your climate before, during and after an examination? How does your internal climate change according to the event, people or your specific perceived needs at the time?

I'm sure at some point in your life you have witnessed great sportsmen and women trying to cross the line and win. It's fascinating to watch their changing emotion as they approach the finishing line. Winning those final closing moments in sport is the hardest thing to do; whether it is a final pot, goal, putt or wicket. From what seemed to be an unassailable winning position, the performer appears to undergo a change in climate; his or her internal weather changes from bright and sunny to dark and gloomy. They don't appear able to find ways of finishing their performance, and appear sad and motionless. It all becomes very serious as thoughts of losing make their way in – 'I'm going to throw it away from this commanding position.' They have simply stopped having fun. Does this ring any bells with you?

Can you remember a time where something you love doing lost its fun and became painful? Do you watch sport eager to see how the situation unfolds? Are you transfixed by the notion of who will handle the pressure and who will crack first? Who can forget the black ball finish in a snooker final, or penalty misses in major championships? Or what about the player who misses a final putt which would have sealed victory for him in a major golf championship?

Whether it is a child at school, an individual at home pursuing a hobby, a high-performing athlete or a business executive, having fun is crucial to our health and happiness.

You will need to pay close attention to whether you put yourself in darkness by drawing the curtains or you put yourself in bright sunlight by pulling the curtains. Either one is your choice. A dark, stormy internal climate is not a good sign of self-care. In contrast, a bright sunny internal climate is fun and shows a high level of self-care. When you are in self-care mode you can do anything. In this state you are capable of doing amazing things.

What happens when things go wrong – what do you do? Do you have an outburst or do you accept the situation and keep having fun? Do you see the funny side? You must strive to generate solutions and change in order to stimulate a light environment and have fun with what you do. In this way you will be able to generate new learning and solutions to the difficulties you may face. Your ability to learn significantly increases if you are having fun. It gives you a unique position to understand how you can generate learning. Every difficult situation is a chance to find the joy out of it.

What can you do to have fun in your life? That is, what really gives you pleasure in life? Do you have fun in a group? Or can you have fun on your own? How does stress impact your ability to have fun? Can you find the fun in the most trying of circumstances? You need a sanity check on how much fun you are having and ensure you are living a value-based perspective.

ABC Plan – 'Having Fun'

Every day is a Saturday

So, by working through your own Awareness, Belief and Correction (ABC) Plan you will be in a better position to see how much fun you are having in your life.

Awareness (A): Fun Attitude

You will need to examine your attitude towards having fun in life. Do you agree or disagree that you have fun while you pursue winning at something? How aware are you of how much fun you have in life? If you are unaware of what enables you to have fun, you will most definitely be operating egotistically or selfishly.

Belief (B): Fun Behaviour

You will need to assess joy in your behaviour. Do you get miserable with significant people while you are doing something important? Are you able to accept your miserable behaviour in life? If you ignore how you behave, you are almost certainly functioning egotistically or selfishly.

Correction (C): Fun Values and Beliefs

You will need to consider how your underlying values and beliefs are about things you dream about and fear in life. You will need to consider how you can align your attitudes, behaviours, values and beliefs in order to embrace fun in your life. If you choose to cultivate an ABC Personal Change Plan you will actively seek to understand how to cultivate more fun in your life. This is an essential self-correction needed to shift your values and beliefs towards winning for the benefit of others. The aim of this process is to shift from a winning for oneself (selfish) to winning for others (selfless) perspective. This will give you a deeper level of joy and contentment.

Are you willing and committed to stop, look and listen to your internal traffic regarding how much fun you are having as you pursue winning in your life?

If yes, it requires reflection and thinking about what thoughts and feelings are invoked when you pursue winning in life.

'Every Day Is a Saturday' Example

I have witnessed, on many occasions, business leaders not having fun in their work. In one case, a CEO – a very caring, charismatic and fun person in the organisation – appeared to be getting more and more sad. Despite this no one had a bad word to say about him as he would continue to consistently help individuals who had problems. He would regularly show his flexibility throughout the organisation. He was strong, open and genuinely supportive to his staff. He was inspirational and clearly won the hearts and minds of staff. Staff were incredibly loyal and followed his values of togetherness. Everyone felt a part of something good as it served a community. The business had started to significantly grow under his leadership and build offices throughout the world. This created significant change and meant that the CEO role was changing. Now he had to lead from a distance, instead of leading through being nearby. He now had to lead a global organisation remotely. This shift in style added a level of complexity over how this should be done. Changes in structures, process and procedures meant that he was not as happy, which impacted on his staff not being as happy. The family aspirations of the business had moved to a more corporate feel. The traditional family values on which the company was built were in conflict with the new desire to become a global corporation. The CEO's usual charismatic nature of wanting to make others happy was reduced as the reality of a global business took over. This made him feel sad as he began to find it difficult to serve others in the way he had done previously.

In conclusion, how much fun you are having has a massive impact on whether others choose to follow you or not. Do you agree? Your reaction or response to having fun indicates your level of selflessness versus selfishness. Do you agree? When you self-correct with the amount of fun you are having with others, how does it make you feel? What are your examples of self-correcting the level of fun you have in your life?

ABC Plan Summary

First, I would like to summarise where we are up to regarding the activities you have performed. In Step One, you have pressed your own TV remote control in order to see how much you listen when you pursue winning in life; what did the data reveal? In Step Two, you began the process of smiling at your errors; what did your errors tell you? In Step Three, you took time to find a Special Place to explore what you avoid in life; what did taking the time to do this reveal? In Step Four, you examined the difference between what you feel and what you do; what did you discover about the degree of separation you experience in life? In this fifth step, you will explore how much fun you are having in life by starting with following questions:

- *How much fun do you have when you are performing and trying to win?*
- *Are you free to express yourself through your performance?*
- *Do you feel alive when you perform?*
- *Do you feel dead when you perform?*
- *Do you feel free to express yourself following an error?*
- *Do you feel happy with your performance?*
- *Do you get excited to perform?*

Step Five: Every Day Is a Saturday

Write a list of twelve hobbies and activities you love doing in your life that make you happy. For example, it might be going to the gym to train or cooking your favourite meal or walking the dog. It doesn't matter what it is so long as you love doing it and you have fun!

Now, arrange your list from your most favourite hobby or activity through to your least favourite hobby or activity.

What do you think of your list? What do significant others think of your list?

Now, arrange a list of work activities from your most favourite to your least favourite. What do you think of your list? How do the lists compare? Are you happy doing your hobbies? Are you happy at work?

What is the biggest difference in your level of happiness across each list? What are your frustrations with your level of happiness at work?

How can you incorporate more of your hobby or activities in your day-to-day work?

What else can you do to improve your fun at work? What can you do to build your hobbies and activities into your work pattern? Better still, what can you do to transform your hobbies into your day-to-day work?

Regardless of whether you are playing sport or in business or education or at home with your family, chasing winning increases the likelihood that you will become selfish. Such selfishness increases our level of misery in life; we feel sad with what we do. Here your desire is to just get through with what you are doing. Our ego takes over, especially when the pressure is on. What is your reaction under pressure? What do you tell yourself? This is your ego operating. In our 'every day is a Saturday' activity you must learn to see the impact the dark side of winning has on your ability to have fun. Do you become more miserable as you strive to win something? In 'every day is a Saturday', consider your thoughts regarding the following questions:

- What was your initial response or reaction to having fun in what you do?

- Do you ignore or hide how miserable you feel at times?
- How do you go about reconciling differences between having fun with your hobbies whilst being unhappy at work?
- Do you resist your differences between feeling happy and feeling sad?
- Does it feel uncomfortable to focus on your happiness in life?
- What does feeling miserable tell you?
- How do you tolerate your unhappiness at work or home?
- How do you behave when you are feeling happy or sad with others in life?
- Are you able to see the kind of things that make you happy?
- What did you discover about your ego by addressing your level of happiness in life?

Fun Mindfulness

Imagine a world where you could just be what you wanted to be with total freedom and fun! Here there was no need for evidence of either being good enough or feeling judged by others. Instead, your best was good enough for all and you didn't feel any negative judgement from others. There was no need to push the boundaries in forging for success. There was no need to push harder, faster or stronger in attempting to achieve something. Instead, it all came naturally through your deep belief in who you are and what you do. Here you are who you want to be, allowing things to occur naturally and accepting all situations and things in your life. Over this **fifth step**, *in shifting from 'doing and fighting' to 'being and allowing', you're happier. If you live by blind faith in your ability rather than proactively seeking evidence, how would you answer the following questions:*

1. *What do you do differently as a result of having blind faith in your life?*
2. *What can you do to maintain being, allowing and accepting instead of doing and fighting at something important?*
3. *How do you go about aligning your differences between what you feel and what you do?*
4. *How does it feel to feel totally competent in what you do?*
5. *How does it feel to not to be negatively judged by others in what you do?*
6. *How do you have fun in this world?*
7. *What do you have to do differently in reality to live more akin to this world?*

So, which way does your coin end up? Do you focus on feeling miserable when you are doing something important? Or do you look to ensure you have fun in your life? Of course you would like to have fun in life. However, you know that at times this is not possible. I have discovered that aligning having fun is vital to increase health and happiness. I have many experiences of helping others have fun in order to improve many elements of their life.

In so doing it creates momentum for others to do the same. Their positive celebration of life reduces fear as they feel more free and happy as a person. This transformation inspires others to do the same and get the most from their life. Having fun with their work is what the best in the world do intuitively. Having no fun puts us into a selfish mode and leads to long-term negative health consequences.

Please select which statement best reflects you when you are about to do something important in life: '*I hated it out there today,*' or, '*I was able to see the good, the bad and ugly of my performance today.*'

Choice 1. 'I hated it out there today'

Miserable mind-set: Being miserable is ego (self importance) focused. Your attention is concentrated on negatively worrying about the outcome of doing something. You will enter a world of fighting using negative thoughts and feelings. You are in flight or fight mode. Here your purpose is survival. You are not enjoying the experience and winning gives you no joy. Life feels dead as you enter yet another wave of chasing winning for survival purposes. In fact, there is no joy at winning, just relief. The level of stress you experience makes you even more miserable and unhappy in what you do. You tell yourself that you have little choice in life. Quality performances are inconsistent. You have a low regard for yourself and see no positives to what you do. You are reactive when faced with problems, which triggers more sad and miserable feelings. You get both frustrated and angry with what you do and those around you. You are very concerned about whether you can come out on top and frightened about what others think.

Choice 2. 'I was able to see the good, the bad and ugly of my performance today'

Fun mind-set: Having a fun mind-set is without ego driven. You are an open vessel as you enter the pursuit of winning. Your attention is centred on having as much fun with what you do as possible. You will enter a world of feeling positive and happy about what your performance can be. You acknowledge and accept negative thoughts and you find a way to minimise their impact, usually through using humour. While you do experience mild stress, it does not trigger a flight or fight response. You have a clear purpose of having fun, making the best of what lies ahead and contributing to something much larger than you. You love what you are doing and winning for others gives you tremendous joy. You feel childlike as you execute your performance, knowing how others will benefit from your work. You are in your element, free and stable doing something you love. You are mindful about how your performance can help your team or community. You feel that you choose everything and consistently deliver quality performances. You have a high regard for yourself and see lots of positives to what you do. You are proactive when problems appear which enables you to find solutions under the most difficult of circumstances. You are both calm and happy with what you do and those around you. You are very relaxed about whether you can come out on top and about what others think.

Conclusion

This miserable versus fun mindfulness allows you to explore your happiness in a much deeper way. By looking at your level of fun when trying to cross the line and win, you will begin to develop a window into your fears when under pressure. You will see the negative impact of what 'you tell yourself' (ego). It will enable you to see how 'miserable' or 'fun-seeking' you are when you want to achieve something important. Can you stop, look and listen to your level of fun in your life? How much commitment to having fun are you prepared to give? Does the pursuit of winning feel like you are in a war or does it feel like you are on a beach holiday?

PART SEVEN

Transformational Ego Programme
(How You Can Serve Others)

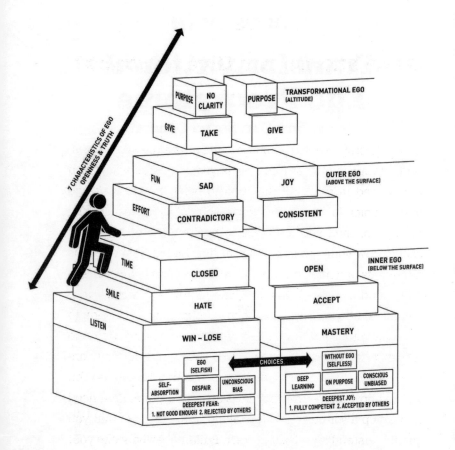

Leadership withoutEGO® Model

22

STEP SIX: Do You Give to Others?

• • •

The sixth step to detox your ego is to answer the above question. If your immediate answer is yes to this question, you are headed in the right direction to being free of your ego and happier in life. If, however, you honestly respond by saying no, then you are open to beginning the process of seeing how your ego impacts your life. Taking from others is dangerous and must change. 'Give' is the sixth characteristic of ego and it shows you how giving to others enhances your emotional freedom. Being open to your immediate reaction to whether you give to others is key to understanding your ego response. This is the sixth step to seeing who you really are and how you can truly benefit from winning for others. You will see how taking from others is an ego response. You need to develop a softness towards taking from others so that you can understand it and self-correct. Building resilience in your life by being softer towards your giving to others is a difficult and time-consuming process.

Your journey starts with a coin flip and a choice.

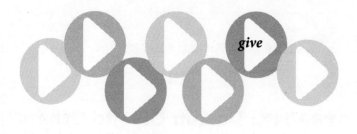

give

Give choice

Whether you know it or not, when you flip your coin of *giving* you have a choice to make. You choose either a 'give' or 'take' mind-set. Whichever side your coin lands on will trigger a self-fulfilling prophecy. That is, you will either give in whatever you do, or you will take from others with what you do.

If you choose not to give in your life, you are choosing an ego reaction. You are choosing to pay attention to and bring fear in your life. This is characterised by the statement: *'I don't get what I want from others.'* Clearly, such a reaction means you are not giving with what you do in life. Taking from others means you will limit your freedom, happiness and success in life.

However, if you are open to understanding your level of giving, you are choosing a selfless response as you begin to find a way to be even more helpful to your community. You are choosing to pay attention to and bring joy in your life. This takes courage and is characterised by the statement: *'I am happy to give to others.'*

By definition, elite athletes who cross the line and become world champions are, at this defining moment, free to give to others, even their opponents. Here, they are free, happy and ready for success in life.

37. STOP: LOOK: LISTEN

Do you give to others?

Or are you willing and committed to stop, look and listen to your internal traffic regarding how much you give to others whilst in pursuit of winning in your life?

If you are, you will need to give unconditionally in your life.

A Personal Experience of Giving

When I think back to my early career, I have come to realise that my cricket experience was a perfect foundation for truly helping others. More than that, the way my career stalled enabled me to understand myself much more deeply so that I could support others with what they do.

I feel incredibly fortunate to be able to help others with what they do. Having pursued my own dreams it is always a privilege to work with people chasing their own dreams. To be building helpful relationships fills me with immense joy and contentment; it's wonderful to serve others by using my experiences – the good, the bad and the ugly. It does seem strange to be using my personal disappointment in cricket to show others how to understand the importance of ego. Whether I'm talking with students, teachers, executives, sports people such as divers, orienteers, snooker players, golfers, footballers and cricketers – it is always a delight to have that quiet informal chat with someone who is unsure of how their selfishness is impacting their choices.

I regard it as a privilege to work within my own sport; driving into Lord's, pulling up to the Grace Gate, heading to Car Park Six, walking through the main pavilion and up the staircase to the home team changing room is always exciting. Donning my team tracksuit and walking back down the staircase through the Long Room, out onto the hallowed Lord's turf, is always a great honour. From my early experiences as a player, to my current involvement as a psychologist, nothing has changed this feeling; being in the role to help others learn how to deal with their ego is very rewarding. My former teammate, now Managing Director of Cricket, has given me full access to working with management, coaches, support staff and players in order to support the collective excellence of the county; he appreciated that gaining the confidence and trust of the staff was essential to my support of the club's ambitions.

As the sun beams across the pitch, it's like being on my favourite beach holiday with my family, and in those moments life couldn't feel sweeter. When I get to the middle of the ground, surveying the stadium, I know I am back at the home of cricket and the place where I started my cricket career over twenty years ago. It's a great feeling; and, while it feels incredible to be able to support others in this environment, I do wonder what would have happened if only I had been supported in the same way all those years ago.

Walking across the outfield and smelling the freshly cut grass, whilst talking to a coach or player, is an amazing experience that I always cherish, and it brings me joy. Back in my playing days, I seemed to have permanently knitted eyebrows and was always so focused; I never smiled, and

I never had fun. It was a serious business and I was serious in my pursuit of winning. I was on a mission and that mission was to fight. I had to win and I took a tough no-compromising approach.

How wrong was I? I didn't appreciate that being 'tough' was so old-fashioned. Instead the modern approach is to be 'soft'. To be open to the moment and explore your emotions for what they are. I didn't do this during my playing days but I have the opportunity to do it now in a new role and it feels so good. Today, with experiences of working with some of the best performers in the world, across many different sports, I am really living my purpose. Any pent-up feelings and worries of being out of control have gone; I feel different about whether I'm good enough, and no longer fear the judgement of others. I have found something to do that really benefits others. I have found my contribution to this world – my true vocation. It is great to relax and enjoy life – it is as good as it gets.

I walk across to the Nursery ground for warm up and nets, a stroll which always generates some interesting chats and discoveries as the coach and players exchange views. You never know what people are going to say before a big game. They may talk about the match and their preparation or just have a general chat about life and their relationships. Alternatively they may just make small talk regarding the weather and the latest sports stories in the papers. Whatever is discussed, it is clear that having a listening ear is the essence of supporting them with their endeavour.

I arrive at the practice area, where some players might ask me to go into the nets and throw them some balls in order to have a bat, while others ask for assistance with their stretching while unravelling certain issues. The beauty of creating chats and having jokes or banter is always so special and I would regularly play-fight or bundle with players with the important aim of relaxing the tense situation and getting them to change direction. Regardless of environment, this is a vital role as I regularly see people *getting in the way of themselves'* with what they do. I see my role as helping people change perspective to reduce the strain and stress of what they are doing. Where did I get such experience to do this, I'd wonder, and immediately reminisce about my experiences on the Nursery ground as a young player, recalling many practices on this miniature area, with its perfect cricket square, and cricket nets in the far left-hand corner.

My team was awash with world-class international players at that time, and I felt extremely privileged and excited about playing alongside them. Bowling at a world champion cricketer, one of my heroes, was one of my life's precious experiences. To be living my dream was pure ecstasy. After an intense period of practice, this world champion would sit us down beside the nets and talk all things cricket. He would describe what was required to play at the highest level and give us feedback about our bowling in the practice session. This was always great fun as I listened intently to every word he said. I was in heaven, and couldn't get enough of what he was saying. Today, I see that experience as the foundation for me helping others. There he was; this immense cricketing icon, taking the time to give to a group of young cricketers – it was a very special moment and one that will live with me forever. How funny life is as such experiences have formed the foundation to my career.

38. STOP: LOOK: LISTEN

What allows you to give to others?

What rich experiences have you had with those who inspire you that you could pass on to others?

Practice would invariably finish back on the Lord's outfield. I would regularly see myself running in and bowling as an eager young man, as if I were having an out-of-body experience, seeing and sensing every movement as if it were happening now. I would then tune back in to what I was doing now; using a baseball mitten, I was acting as a wicketkeeper to catch each ball from the bowlers running in and mimicking what they were about to do in the match. It is always great fun, especially as sometimes the opposition fast bowlers would ask to join in so that they could bowl a few deliveries. I always kept on my toes and enjoyed being helpful to all those playing. Fielding practice would finish by conducting both long and short fielding drills. It is such a great environment and so inspiring.

I can honestly say that regardless of the environment I'm in I can always find the joy in mucking in and helping others, whether I'm in a classroom or boardroom, poolside, up a remote mountain, in a snooker club, or on a golf course or a football pitch or a cricket field. Getting stuck into the environment of others always feels the right thing to do, especially if it's back at the home of cricket – a place where it all started for me.

Giving in Business

Helping executives to unconditionally give more to each other is always fascinating, and I've had many discussions with executives about unconditional giving in the workplace. Sometimes I'm faced with executives who think I'm joking and get defensive; at other times, it stimulates lots of discussion and debate. I can immediately see which executives are sufficiently open to their emotional pain by the way they give to each other; it's always a rewarding experience for me to observe. More so than on the occasions I have witnessed when executives clash due to not giving to each other and simply being selfish.

Taking from Others and Poor Business Performance

For example, in one situation I was engaged to help resolve a significant conflict involving a director and her two managers within a global financial firm. Talking to all parties to examine the context of their work revealed a lot about the level of selfishness in this situation. On the one hand, the director was pushing each of her managers for extra information regarding how they were doing business as a result of her boss wanting more detail, and becoming frustrated with both their overt and covert reluctance to give the information required. On the other hand, the managers felt stifled by the extra close attention and scrutiny. They simply wanted to continue to work as they had always done and didn't appreciate what they perceived as a command-and-control leadership style. For them, their manager wasn't giving unconditionally.

Added to this, they also blamed the director and her selfish style for one of their colleagues leaving. Neither party spoke openly about their frustrations and clearly each party was unhappy. The relationships became strained and at times unbearable. One manager handed in a resignation letter that completely shocked and upset the director. From her perspective, she couldn't understand why she was being treated so badly by her staff, as she thought she was giving. This only increased her perceived stress as her boss wanted to know why her staff were leaving, which she felt reflected poorly on her leadership. This added further complexity as her boss's extra attention on her business unit was also significantly making her look at things from a different perspective.

I was able to help raise the awareness of the need for each party to give more to each other. Conducting both individual and group meetings we were able to unravel some of the selfishness at play. What was going on in emotional terms? Both parties began to realise the way they were looking at the issue and both parties accepted that there were unintended consequences for their entrenched attitudes and behaviour. The director felt cold-shouldered by her managers, especially the staff member who had offered her resignation; while the managers felt the director was increasingly becoming autocratic and selfish, impacting their ability to do their jobs as she focused on getting more business data. They also appreciated their relationship had significantly suffered as a result of losing one of their closest friends. They began to accept that it wasn't their director's fault. An open dialogue revealed a range of emotion from frustration to anger to humour regarding their differences.

The director came to realise that she had increasingly

thrown herself into work since her father had become seriously ill. It was evident that she was not aware she was placing more attention on trying to control her business. This was the first time she had spoken about what had been going on in her personal life in the workplace. It was great to see her become more insightful and open as she considered why she was pushing her managers so hard. It was clear that she was glad to be more open but she also appeared nervous and vulnerable about what she was giving and what the process was going to yield. Privately she realised she was closed to the reality of her difficult personal situation by working even harder. When her work began to demand extra information, her response was to become more transactional in order to maintain some perceived stability in her life. She hadn't realised how much her lack of giving impacted her style and her managers. The director accepted her personal stress, which helped her to relax more. She decided to put a plan together to increase the level of openness and give more across her team and the office.

This started by talking through, with her managers, her difficult situation with her father's illness. She also gave them an explanation of why their colleague left. She became more aware of how her father's illness was impacting her judgement. Again, her managers, on witnessing the authenticity of what she was saying, began to soften and gain greater empathy for her personal situation. They expressed sorrow for ignoring her and making life difficult. They accepted their friend left due to other circumstances. Both parties appeared relieved. There was an instant correction and alignment about how the office could work better and recover its position. As fear on both sides started to ebb away, they started to collaborate and plan a better way of working. Firstly, a series of additional kick-off weekly meetings were arranged that include the managers, making them much happier. One manager instantly responded by withdrawing their resignation, to the delight of the director; while the other made suggestions about how they could create a better office culture by being more open and working more closely together. The director gained feedback regarding her style and accepted this wasn't a criticism of her leadership and business acumen.

 39. STOP: LOOK: LISTEN

How do you cope when someone consistently demands from you?

Are you able to give more time and energy to a demander?

She instantly became more relaxed and softened her approach towards her managers. As they revealed more, both parties were eager to highlight what they needed from each other. Each party realised the need to improve their relationships by giving more to each other. This was the first time both parties had spoken directly to each other. With regular weekly meetings conducted off-site over breakfast, both issues were discussed so that they could get to the office together and debrief their teams accordingly and from a united front. The director gave the managers more autonomy, while the managers gave greater levels of feedback to the director about what their needs were moving forward. The office recorded a significantly improved performance as all parties grew in confidence as they became more open. Frustrations were more frequently aired and an emphasis on winning for the team became the norm. A greater level of togetherness resulted in increased happiness and performance.

In conclusion, this conflict situation was a result of self-ishness. Here the ego of both parties became rigid, stuck and didn't give to each other. When openness and giving on each side was stimulated, their differences and misalignment began to be resolved and fade. They appeared to like and respect each other. Clearly, talking was the birthplace for a better way of working.

Below is an outline example of an ABC Plan for an interna-tional cricket coach. It will highlight how the individual was able to make a significant change in aligning his thinking and action to achieve more. This individual became aware of how not giving impacted his pursuit of winning in his life at the moment of achieving his best ever cricket coaching. Such an example will highlight our selfishness or self-importance as he began to create a feeling of giving.

My ABC Plan Example: An International Cricket Coach

It's a bright sunny day, and I'm at a local farm with an international cricket coach who, following his early exit from the professional game, has been coaching for most of his life. Fortunate enough to have played first class cricket for Somerset, and to have represented England at under-19 level, he had the privilege of playing with the greats, like Sir Ian Botham, Sir Viv Richards and Steve Waugh. When his playing career came to an end, he found his true vocation as a full-time cricket coach. Having been through the coaching system as a player, as a coach he feels he can give helpful feedback in this area. Over the last twenty years, he has developed a very unique and distinctive approach to helping players understand their way of playing.

Today he works privately as a specialist technical batting coach for a number of first class and international players as well as running his own Cricket Academy that gets young players to understand the quality standards required to become elite pro cricketers.

Although he has a high-calibre history, for whatever reason, his ideas have fallen on deaf ears within the system. No one took him seriously and the authorities simply rejected his ideas. The harder he tried, the worse it got as his approach to cricket coaching was dismissed. He had hit a brick wall in his career. He was totally demoralised and this ate away at his self-esteem; his only solution was to build a Cricket Academy offering his ideas to aspiring players. Here, young players got the opportunity to expand on his ideas over long time frames. Some of his graduates produced some amazing results and became first class cricketers. He began to develop an acute awareness for detail in the art of batting, understanding the subtle changes required in the way someone plays the game. He had an eye for the symmetry and alignment required by each player, based not only on his experience of playing with great players but also on his own natural ability having played first team cricket at the age of fourteen. Over the years, he realised that by finding a community to give his ideas to he truly felt he could contribute to the game. This gave him a deep sense of nourishment, identity and self-care.

However, he still craved the recognition and support from others in the game. It was difficult for him to reconcile his unique approach to how significant others in the game perceived him. He was very frustrated and unhappy at not being able to access higher levels of the game.

1: Awareness

My aim was to help him see his situation from a very different perspective. We began by discussing the following statements: which statement best reflects you – *'I always take from others,'* or, *'I happily give to others'*?

He then began to tell me all about his giving to others. He expressed strong views of how he went about helping others over his whole career, listing story after story about giving to others and explaining that he was in a giving role. He fervently presented a strong case for giving more than he received. Clearly, he appeared frustrated, even angry, that others were not giving back to him. I asked him to give some instances, so he expanded on specific examples of different people he has helped over the years and how unfair life was regarding what he was getting back. After he had finished what felt like an extended rant, he asked me for my opinion.

I asked him if he was honestly prepared to be open and committed to exploring what I was about to say. He nodded. I then proceed to tell him that from where I was sitting he took more than he gave. This enraged him. He totally disagreed, and became instantly defensive. He sat quite rigid, maintaining his position that he felt hard done by: 'What makes you say that after what I've just said?'

'Well,' I replied, 'clearly, on the surface you have been giving your entire career. However, below the surface I see something different going on.'

'What?' he said. 'What are you talking about?'

'Your giving appears conditional on what you get back from others. Are you totally happy with giving?' I asked. His initial response was, of course, but when I pressed him a little harder, he began to think about it. It became clear to him that he wasn't truly happy with giving freely. Naturally I asked why and he responded that he felt harshly treated by others in the game and that his skills and abilities were not being recognised. He spoke about the difficulties he was having with certain people in the game and explained that he felt blocked out of opportunities to coach at a higher level. I asked if there was any benefit to being blocked by others. He firmly replied, 'No,' to which I disagreed and said there must be some benefit or you wouldn't hold your position on it. He pondered this. While he did so, I asked him about the questions he constantly referred to, such as, 'Why am I always on the outside?' and 'Why can't I get in?' He was stunned into silence. There was no speaking for several minutes. He was quiet and deeply thoughtful.

I began to dig deeper by suggesting that he was the one rejecting himself first and that his ego was not allowing him to see this. He was reeling with this news but was clearly more reflective than defensive. His position softened as he began to accept the perspective. He asked if I could expand in order to clarify and understand what I was saying as he was beginning to accept his flaw.

From a deeper perspective, he had learnt to pay attention to feeling rejected. This in turn shaped what he chose to tell himself (his ego) and as a consequence, he unknowingly invited rejection into his own personal way of thinking and behaving.

We went over his previous stories and he began linking what I was saying with his own recall of events. He began seeing how his perception of being a victim supported his view of being on the outside of the game. He began to see how his own contribution to being rejected by others was working in his life. He wanted to know how he could reconcile this flaw.

2: Belief

On the surface, he was suffering rejection from others while below the surface he was inadvertently choosing rejection himself. This was a lightbulb moment. The notion of seeing is believing came true in an instant. He immediately accepted his own part in his own rejection. He started to explore and accept other experiences of rejection in life. This was a liberating experience where his perceived pain, of feeling on the outside, was revealed. Unravelling his grievances was a long and exhaustive process but very enlightening and enabling. Next we talked about how he could create a self-correction plan to feel more included than excluded and gain the recognition he desired.

3: Correction

With this newfound awareness and acceptance he began the process of self-correction. How could he begin to think about winning for the benefit of others to reduce his anxiety about feeling rejected? His solution was to think about giving his technical expertise freely to the national game. This allowed him to assess his own style and improve his own way of engaging others by feeling more in than out with significant others. An illustration of this was he felt able to go directly to people he wanted to interact with. Here he was able to phone, email or text international world-class players directly instead of previously going through a third person. So he stopped sending letters to a third person hoping they would pass them on. He accepted that he had to convert his feeling of being on the outside with others to a feeling of being on the inside with others. The significant shift was that he was beginning to understand that in order to receive he had to give to others first. In other words he needed to shift from selfish, victim-led thinking to selfless, hero-led thinking. We designed a plan of giving to the game at the highest level.

This led to him offering his work to the national system. He began eagerly watching international world-class players to see how he could help. He would also travel around the country to demonstrate his coaching innovation to the national batting coaches. He would present at coaches' conferences, openly giving ideas about batting drills and areas to modernise the game. He showed his innovations in batting to the national women's team coach. He worked with three players to improve their form as well as providing in-house training for other professional coaches.

He also went on the road, showing his coaching ideas to many professional county clubs. He freely gave the paperwork, presentations, drills, videos and training programme to national representatives. He then had the chance to help two international players, which he did over a short-term basis. He saw significant improvement in their play but felt like he didn't get the recognition. Unfortunately even given this level of activity he still felt on the outside and rejected until one day where he was given an opportunity to work with an international cricket captain. He was very excited at the prospect of helping a player on the world stage.

The Defining Moment

Having taken many years to observe this international captain batting, he was now perfectly positioned to advise him on making some technical adjustments that could make a significant impact on his performance. He had seen some fundamental issues with the way this captain batted and at last he was being utilised by the captain who went on to score significant Test-winning performances for his country. It was a proud moment all round. Since then, this International coach has been invited to technically coach another world-class International cricket captain.

Your ABC Plan: Giving Unconditionally

You need to ask yourself the following questions: do you give to others in life? Or do you take from others in life?

If you have answered yes to both of these questions, then this is the paradox you face. On one hand, you may feel you are open and available to others, while on the other, you may feel threatened or judged by others. As a result, whether wittingly or unwittingly, you retreat into yourself. Here you are not being kind to yourself. You are experiencing low levels of self-care and so you may find it difficult to give to others when you are not kind to yourself. When are you kind to yourself? At what times do you feel like withdrawing from others?

Here you pay attention to being quiet. In fact, you may feel irritated by people and this natural tendency to pull back from others means you have low interpersonal skills. Here you are not getting what you want from others. You are operating on ego and fear. Having a starting position of 'taking from others' drains your emotional and intellectual energies. Taking from others distracts you and prevents you from enjoying life. This is dangerous and must stop. You will need to accept and shift away from taking from others for gains to be made. Being open to developing empathy and a greater care for others is key.

Do you want to change?

Can you develop a series of activities that involve others? What activities and hobbies can you do that enhance your involvement with others? Giving to others stimulates freedom and happiness, but requires you to develop your interpersonal skills. By giving to others you are building up a readiness to receive. You will need a high level of self-care in order to receive from someone else. You also need a high level of self-care to forgive others. What do you receive from others? How can you forgive others? Do you find it difficult to forgive others?

Being relational and giving helps to reduce fear and buried emotional pain in your life. What are your relationships like? Do you find it difficult or easy to develop strong relationships with others? Are they growing or diminishing in your company? How are you proactively building your relationships with others?

There are four key elements to building relations. First, you need to be more direct with others about what affects you. I have used 'I feel . . . sad . . . mad . . . frustrated . . .' etc. to explain my position to others. This non-threatening way of starting a sentence ensures that the recipient processes my view without us descending into a blame culture. It places the emphasis on your to sort you own emotional pain out before potentially creating an outburst from others. As a result, issues can be aired and relations built. Secondly, finding some common ground to share with another person means you can deepen your relationships. For example, you might collect fine art and being able to discuss this with someone else who also shares in your passion develops your relationship with them. Thirdly, you can spend time in different environments with the person you want to build a relationship with; for example, you can go to a sports event or out to dinner with someone with whom you want to build a relationship with. In this way you can cement the quality of your relationship with others. Finally, sharing power in your relationships is critical to improving their form and shape. If there is an inequality of power, it is very difficult to develop quality relationships.

In summary, it is clear that giving is important to cleanse your selfishness or ego. It will take commitment and willingness if gains are to be made and you are able to lavish honour in your environment.

ABC Plan – Unconditional Giving to Others

Understanding your demanding behaviour

So, by working through your own Awareness, Belief and Correction (ABC) Plan you will be in a better position to see how much you give to others in your life.

Awareness (A): Give Attitude

You will need to examine your attitude towards giving in life. Do you agree or disagree that you take more than you give in your pursuit of winning at something? How aware are you of unconditional giving in life? If you are unaware of what you give to others, you will most definitely be operating egotistically or selfishly.

Belief (B): Give Behaviour

You will need to assess and believe what you see about your giving behaviour. Do you ignore giving to significant people while you are doing something important? Are you able to accept your taking behaviour in life? If you ignore how you behave, you are almost certainly functioning egotistically or selfishly.

Correction (C): Give Values and Beliefs

You will need to consider what your underlying values and beliefs are about what you give and take in life. You will need to consider how you can align your attitudes, behaviours, values and beliefs in order to embrace what you give to others in life. If you choose to cultivate an ABC Personal Change Plan you will actively seek to understand unconditional giving in your life. This is an essential self-correction needed to shift your values and beliefs towards winning for the benefit of others. The aim of this process is to shift from a winning for oneself (selfish) to winning for others (selfless) perspective. This will give you a deeper level of joy and contentment.

Are you willing and committed to stop, look and listen to your internal traffic regarding how much you give while you pursue winning in your life?

If yes, it requires reflection and thinking about what thoughts and feelings are invoked when you give to others unconditionally.

Unconditional Giving to Others' Example

Helping executives to give more unconditionally to

other individuals is fantastic experience. Supporting leaders build their organisations through developing their teams of people is always very rewarding. Below are a couple of examples:

- Developing teams of architects and engineers to significantly improve their delivery on building projects by learning how to give more to each other on the outset of a project. Here I helped the Group CEO of this property and construction company increase his ability to get such disciplines (as well as other disciplines) to work more effectively together. Each team selected specific executives to the interdisciplinary leaders' group within the business. This group was tasked with designing a new set of procedures, processes and protocols that represented a new way of working together. The aim was to stimulate and increase the company's ability to develop a work culture of individual expertise and collective excellence.

- Supporting various sales directors get more from their staff by helping them enhance their ability to give unconditionally. In IT, this meant specifically helping a leader give even more to a number of direct reports who were very difficult people. In recruitment, this evolved through the leadership development programme aimed at helping executives to build on their ability to select, train and develop the right people for the right roles. In so doing these leaders were better able to build greater role clarity and maximise decision-making. The programme focused on leaders developing their ability to 'give' more to their staff so that they could develop a critical mass of staff who shared their values and work ethic around caring for others.

- Helping a retail director to give more unconditionally to his buyers so that they executed better performances. This meant that staff felt more support in the sales process from purchasing stock to the goods being sold out in the various high street stores. His passion for supporting, networking and sharing with others ensured he could add greater value throughout the sales process. His customers immediately felt he cared for their business as if it were his own. This led to a deepening of his customer relationships, which in turn helped to spur new orders in new markets such as online retailing.

All these groups, and many others, came to the realisation that selfishness with their work led to poor relationships and poor results. While this is not new, all the executives had a new framework for deepening their relationships that led to a better way of working. They were able to see how they could make the shift towards a more selfless state. Being able to engender greater empathy and genuinely serve others led to significantly higher performance. In these examples the ability to 'give to others' was key to improving and sustaining not only the health but also the profit of the organisation.

By serving others these leaders ensured they influenced and got what they wanted from their teams. In contrast, I have regularly witnessed many executives not getting what they want from others. Here they choose to feel 'out' rather than 'in' with others and their organisation. Such executives feel isolated and excluded, especially when it comes to engaging with their bosses. They feel ignored and not a part of what is happening. In these circumstances, every day is frustrating and such individuals just operate on autopilot. They become increasingly sad about their situation but don't know how to resolve it. This leads to more counterproductive attitude and behaviour and potential sabotage or thoughts about leaving. I have seen many good executives choose to exit their company because they feel taken for granted. In most cases, their lack of emotional insight meant they were unwittingly making an uninformed choice. In these cases, these leaders needed to become aware of their emotional despair. They chose to see it themselves as being drained by others' exploitation.

It was as if they had kept their battery on and now the life was slowing draining away. They were running on empty and began to tell themselves there was only one option left – to leave. This framework enabled them to become much more informed about their emotional world and how they viewed themselves and their career. Organisations need to accept and correct how their staff may be feeling in order to ensure that they do everything in their power to make sure staff are optimal.

ABC Plan Summary

First, I would like to summarise where we are up to regarding the activities you have performed. In Step One, you have pressed your own TV remote control in order to see how much you listen when you pursue winning in life; what did the data reveal? In Step Two, you began the process of smiling at your errors; what did you errors tell you? In Step Three, you took time to find a Special Place to explore what you avoid in life; what did taking the time to do this reveal? In Step Four, you examined the difference between what you feel and what you do; what did you discover about the degree of separation you experience in life? In Step Five, you explored how much fun you are having in life; what did you discover about yourself regarding how much fun you have? In this sixth step, you will explore how much you give to others in life by starting with following questions:

- *How much do you give to others when you are performing and trying to win?*
- *Are you free to give to others through your performance?*
- *Do you enjoy giving when you perform?*
- *Do you enjoy taking when you perform?*
- *Do you see the benefit of giving to others?*
- *Do you feel happy with giving to others?*
- *Do you get excited to give?*

Step Six: Unconditional Giving to Others

- *What do you do for others?*
- *How unconditional is your act of giving?*
- *Take some time to think about how it makes you feel to give to others.*
- *Write a list of six people you have strong relationships with. These can be family members, friends, clients and colleagues. Beside each name specifically list what you give to them and what they give to you.*
- *What are the differences in the level of giving and taking?*
- *Is there a pattern?*
- *How does seeing what you give to others and take from others feel?*
- *Now, write a list of six people you have poor relationships with. These can be family members, friends, clients and colleagues. Beside each name specifically list what you give to them and what they give to you.*
- *What are the differences in the level of giving and taking?*
- *Is there a pattern?*
- *How does seeing what you give to others and take from others feel?*
- *What are the differences between the good and poor relationships in terms of giving and taking?*
- *What can you do to improve the amount of giving on both lists? Why do you have good and poor relationships? Is it possible to treat everyone the same by giving more unconditionally to all?*

Regardless of whether you are playing sport or in business or education or at home with your family, chasing winning increases the likelihood that you will take rather than give. Such selfishness increases our level of taking from others in life; we feel others owe us. Here your desire is to get what you need from others. This is our ego taking over and it occurs especially when the pressure is on. What do you give when the pressure is on? What do you tell yourself? This is your ego operating. In the 'unconditional giving' activity you must learn to see the impact the dark side of winning has on your ability to give. Do you take from others as you strive to win something? In the 'unconditional giving' activity, consider your thoughts regarding the following questions:

- What was your initial response or reaction to giving more to others in what you do?
- Do you ignore or hide how much you give and take from others?
- How do you go about reconciling differences between giving and taking from others?
- Do you resist your differences between giving and taking?
- Does it feel uncomfortable to focus on what you give and take from your relationships in life?
- What does giving tell you?
- How do you tolerate others taking from you at work or home?
- How do you behave when you are giving to others in life?

- Are you able to see the kind of things that make you want to give?
- What did you discover about your ego by addressing your level of giving in life?

Give Mindfulness

Imagine a world where every thought, word or action you did enabled others to feel totally energised, free and happy! Here there are no individuals demanding from you. Instead, everyone gives everyone else positive feedback and praise. No negative judgement exist. Every conversation is inspiring and you live to give to others in order to meet their needs. Everyone feels encouraged to be the best that they can be. Over this sixth step, you are invited to shift from a negative 'taking from others' mind-set to a positive 'giving to others' mind-set. If you were living by a creed of unconditional giving in this world, how would you answer the following questions:

1. *What do you do differently as a result of unconditional giving in your life?*
2. *What can you do to maintain a positive non-judging and giving mind-set, instead of a negative judging and taking mind-set?*
3. *How do you go about shifting from a 'take from others' to a 'give to others' mind-set?*
4. *How does it feel to be totally supported by others in what you do?*
5. *How does it feel to not be negatively judged by others in what you do?*

6. *How do you go about giving to others in this world?*

7. *What would you have to do in order to make this world a reality?*

So, which way does your coin end up? Do you focus on giving or taking when you are doing something important? Of course you would like to give more in life. However, you know that at times this is not possible. I have discovered that giving to others more is vital to increase health, happiness and purpose. I have many experiences of seeing others give more and improve many elements of their life. In so doing it creates momentum for others to do the same. Their giving reduces fear as they feel more free and happy as a person. This transformation inspires others to do the same and get the most from their life. Giving to others is what the best in the world do intuitively. Taking from others puts us into a selfish mode and leads to long-term negative health consequences.

Please select which statement best reflects you when you are about to do something important in life: '*I always demand from others*,' or, '*I always give to others.*'

Choice 1. 'I always demand from others'

Take mind-set: Focusing on taking from others is ego (self-importance) driven. You place your attention on what you can take from others. You lack empathy for others as you are too self-centred on what you need. Here your aim is to get what you need from others before they start to take from you. You enjoy the power and control it gives you as you can clearly influence and persuade others to do things for you. You feel good about taking from others. This leads to a mind-set of taking from everyone around you. You are prepared to show annoyance if you don't get what you want from others. You work hard to manipulate those people. Your performance is inconsistent as you are more concerned with what others are doing and saying. Your confidence is affected when you don't get what you want from others. You refuse to be judged by others.

Choice 2. 'I always give to others'

Give mind-set: Focusing on giving to others is without ego driven. You are eager to give to others in order that they flourish. You are open to receiving back from others as well. This makes you well balanced and stable with the things you do. You have a vision and a value for giving to others, as you are aware that your bigger purpose in life is to support your team or community. You are ambitious about what others can do and how they can impact you and your community. You get immense pleasure out of learning from what you give. You see giving as a priority and an important part of your performance. Others are inspired by your giving and begin to think differently about their own level of giving. They see the freedom and energy from trying to win for others and they are keen to learn to be the same way. There is a greater appreciation of responding in the right way to others who selfishly take. You are excited by the challenge of giving more in life. Giving to others is perceived as natural and you accept that it is a fundamental part of understanding your purpose in life. You gain immense joy out of finding your purpose in life through how you serve others.

Conclusion

In conclusion, how do you react or respond to giving and taking from others? Are you consistent in how you give and take? What you choose has a massive impact on whether others choose to follow you or not. Do you agree? Your reaction or response to giving and taking indicates your level of selflessness versus selfishness. Do you agree? When you self-correct your level of giving to others, how does it make you feel?

What are your examples of self-correcting your giving in your life?

23

STEP SEVEN: Do You Have a Purpose in Life?

· · ·

The seventh step to detox your ego is to answer the above question. If your immediate answer is yes to this question, you are headed in the right direction to being free of your ego and happier in life. If, however, you honestly respond by saying no, then you are open to beginning the process of seeing how your ego impacts your life. Being open to your immediate reaction to whether you know your purpose in life is key to understanding your ego response. Having no clarity about what you do is dangerous and must change.'Purpose' is the seventh characteristic of ego and it shows you how choosing no direction in your life is a way of hiding your emotional pain. This is the seventh and final step to seeing who you really are and how you can truly benefit from winning for others. You will see how a lack of purpose is a selfish act in life. You will see whether you have clarity about what you do in life. You will understand that having a lack of clarity about your purpose is an ego response. You need to develop a softness towards what your purpose is in order to understand it and self-correct. Building resilience in your life by being softer towards what your purpose in life is, is a difficult and time-consuming process.

Your journey starts with a coin flip and a choice.

purpose

Purpose Choice

Whether you know it or not, when you flip your coin of *purpose* you have a choice to make. You choose either a 'purpose' or 'no purpose' mind-set. Whichever side your coin lands on will trigger a self-fulfilling prophecy. That is, you will either follow a purpose in whatever you do or you will have no real direction in what you do.

If you choose not to have clarity of direction in your life, you are choosing an ego reaction. You are choosing to pay attention to fear in your life. This is characterised by the statement: *'I do not know what my purpose in life is.'* Clearly, such a reaction means you are not following a purpose with what you do in life. Having no direction means you will limit your freedom, happiness and success in life.

However, if you are open to understanding your direction in life, you will understand that the ultimate purpose of your life is to serve others. Here you are choosing a selfless response as you begin to give even more to your team or community. In so doing, you will become clearer on what your purpose is in life. You are choosing to pay attention to joy in your life. This takes courage and is characterised by the statement: *'I know what my purpose in life is.'*

40. STOP: LOOK: LISTEN

Do you know your purpose?

If so, paying attention to the positive feedback from giving others will shed light on your true purpose in life?

Are you willing and committed to stop, look and listen to your internal traffic regarding serving others as a way to understand what your true purpose in life is?

If you are, you will be choosing to live your dream.

By definition, elite athletes who cross the line and become world champions are, at this defining moment, clear on their purpose in life. Here they are free, happy and ready for success in life.

A Personal Experience of Purpose

How funny life is. I feel I've come full circle – back to working with the sport I have always loved: cricket. However, there is a dramatic difference between how I manage my inner voice, my relationships and how I try to influence others. Some would say that this is just a sign of a maturing individual. However, I feel it is more about being aware of my own selfishness. You need to consider what choices you are making regarding whether you are being selfish or selfless as you pursue winning in life. This will be a pivotal moment as you explore how you think, feel and behave in your life.

Not fulfilling my potential in my cricket career was perfect for making me able to see my own selfishness. Being an under-achiever helped me to understand my own buried emotional pain and really understand the 'cause and effect' underlying my insecurities, inadequacies and low self-esteem. I could see the choices I was making in my emotional world that meant I always had the feeling that something was miss-ing with my game. I discovered that this 'missing something' was a lack of understanding about the emotional pain I had experienced in life. Things were beginning to fall into place and I was beginning to feel a lot freer and happier. This was the great irony; I had lost the opportunity to play the sport I loved but I had gained the chance to use my disappointment to help others. I found this strange at first until I began to process the significance of becoming a better, more rounded person as I started helping others. I began to understand a lot of my competitiveness in sport was ego-driven and a result of misalignment between my values for fairness and what was actually happening in my life.

I was able to use my acceptance of a lack of fairness to support others to clear their own internal traffic so that they could behave in a responsible and accountable way. I soon realised that this was what I had to do – it was my mission in life. My true purpose for living was not to be that cricketing hero I'd always dreamt of being. Instead, it was to use my experiences of underachieving in cricket to help those more able than me to achieve more. As I've pursued serving oth-ers, I've had so many experiences of complete joy witnessing others achieve their ultimate dreams. It was as if I'd been watching one of my sons or my daughter do something for the first time – like ride their bike or swim. Watching them learn something new is so rewarding. I can picture those experiences, and the thing that comes to my mind every time is the depth of my euphoric feelings. On each and every occasion the feeling of watching someone achieve a lifetime's dream was more ecstatic than me achieving my own dreams of playing professional cricket. Really? I would regularly ask myself how could this be? Over time I have come to realise there is just something more special in emotional terms supporting someone else to live his or her dream. I am always surprised at this even though I've experienced it on lots of occasions over the years.

If you think about using your gifts to help others, then you will fulfil your potential as you begin to understand what your purpose in life is. It rewards you emotionally and heals any unnecessary emotional anxiety you may have. Here you are purposeful, aligned and living your life for the benefit of others.

I discovered that if an individual is focused on self-importance (what we tell ourselves) in their pursuit of winning, they are more likely to be embroiled in psychological battle. In contrast, if the individual has a clear picture about how he or she could help others as they chase winning, they appear to reduce their internal psychological battles. Consequently, I have found that if the latter is true, then they get immersed in mastery of skills and relationships and therefore influence others more wholeheartedly. The key here is to ask the following question: how can you serve others when you are doing something important?

This gives you the chance to shift from a selfish to a self-less state. In a selfless state you automatically increase your freedom, happiness and success. Here you have a greater purpose beyond yourself while increasing the intensity on the personal meaning of what you are doing. I have found that encouraging people to think about their role in serving others whilst they pursue their dreams boosts something special in their life. If the individual gets the blend of self-ishness versus selflessness right you naturally see consistent advanced growth for the person. Over the years, across my different environments, I have discovered many people sustain high performance and happiness.

What became obvious is that something changes for these individuals when they became more selfless in what they do. I found that for several elite athletes who became world champions, their thinking was completely different to what you would expect. It provided confusing, complex and even counterintuitive data. These elite athletes became acutely aware that the mind-set that took them to world-class level was inadequate for becoming the best in the world. There was a realisation, either wittingly or unwittingly, that to become a world champion required, at that defining moment, a completely different way of thinking.

Reaching the Summit with a World Champion

It was interesting to see that something else was needed to cross the line as a world champion; and this was the paradox that I have already referred to in this book, the World Champion Contradiction.

What had enabled them to get to such a high level was ineffective in helping them become a world champion. A paradoxical conclusion: the traditional attributes associated with reaching the top were a selfish ruthlessness and obsession with winning, neither of which was helpful in crossing the line at world championship level. Instead, advance growth required new thinking. It was as if the person had climbed the highest mountain in the world and was just short of the summit. This extreme environment was at altitude – there was significantly less oxygen for breathing. It therefore demanded the individual become more aware of their surroundings, and what it took to get to the summit when there was less oxygen present. Here they needed to appreciate the enormity of putting one step in front of the other. They needed to sip the air in order not to waste the short supply of oxygen. Importantly, the situation demanded that they think of their safety in numbers, working together so they all got to the summit. Individuals who worked alone were in danger. There was greater risk in isolation at altitude. There needed to be a mind-set of helping each other as a community if they were to limit potential death and get to the summit.

This is true of elite athletes striving to become world champions. For those who understood how becoming a world champion can really serve others, there was an easy way of achieving it. Those individuals who did not see the bigger picture, and centred the execution of their task on themselves, imploded and came up short. Their selfishness didn't help them achieve a life-long dream – becoming the best in the world is only achieved from a standpoint of 'how can I serve others with my achievement?' Such athletes understand they have a deeper purpose underlying their success in life. Such athletes make a significant shift from 'it's all about me winning' to 'it's all about how my winning can help others'. In cricket, examples like Sir Viv Richard and Sachin Tendulkar realised the importance of becoming a world champion for their respective nations. They had increased responsibility and personal meaning in what they were doing. They had a bigger purpose. As a result, they were free to express themselves fully at the most important times. They got completely 'out of the way of themselves'.

It is a shame that I did not have such a perspective when I played cricket, so I never got the chance to reflect in this way. However, I am able to see how helpful it is to others now. From what starts out as a friendly chat the person would walk away feeling much better, having had the chance to discuss things from a new angle and talk about things that were generally left unspoken. Everyone I speak with enjoys such an encounter to talk things through. You might be a parent, teacher or student; an executive, doctor or athlete; a friend, family member or colleague. Regardless of who you are, this new perspective gives you a new lens to look through regarding how you pursue winning in life.

Finding Purpose in Business

Helping executives to face the question of their purpose in life is always very interesting and rewarding. I have had many discussions with senior executives about what constitutes purpose in life, especially whilst away on one of the Leadership withoutEGO® retreats where we spend the whole day discussing purpose and legacy. Sometimes this is easy as they contemplate their lot and their direction in life. You can always see the cogs turning as they instantly want to make a change and consider how they are going to retire and exit the business. This is a difficult process for the most able in our society. Therefore it is great to learn from them and see how they go about planning life after they retire. Such individuals explore how to better have an impact on the world they live in. Others receive the purpose question with bewilderment and surprise as they automatically assume that they are already living with purpose. However, when questioned about what legacy they are leaving and how their skills are benefitting others, a puzzled or blank expression takes over as they realise superficial answers won't do. Instead, they are invited to explore how they can genuinely use their skills to serve others in order that they find their true purpose in life. This always stimulates much discussion and debate about their life and how their skills should be utilised for the benefit of others. Helping executives understand their leadership gifts and how to clarify their purpose is always tough but inspiring.

Over the years I have supported many board executives to better understand what they want from their careers. I have spent time helping them to clarify their purpose in life. For example, I helped an MD to rediscover his passion for inspiring others. He had been entrepreneurial for most of his career but with changes in the business climate his role became much more pressurised and dissatisfying. Changes from how he reported global figures to having the elbow room to make local decisions all impacted on whether he felt he was doing a meaningful job.

Through our discussion he was able to reawaken and recalibrate his passion for helping others. He began to realise that he had moved away from what brought him happiness in the workplace. He began to process the huge level of stress being passed down by his boss and you could see him wondering if it was worth it. Discussions led on to what his ideal role would be in life. This included chatting round what legacy he would like to leave behind. These were deep and reflective conversations that stimulated a different way of thinking. He became aware of his passion for new technology and how it could be developed both commercially and through connecting different people he had met over his career. He began to feel alive again and had insight into what he was good at. It was clear that he was going through some form of transition and wanted more from his role.

He began to accept that while on the one hand he had a great position within a global company that met the needs of his family, on the other hand, he wanted more purpose and meaning from his day-to-day work. He appeared both tired and frustrated at not completing a whole job. He was questioning what his value was in the overall picture of things. Change was being stirred. Following many meetings and discussions on what he really wanted to do, he started to put a plan together to build a bridge from his current actual situation to a brighter, preferred state. This included being open with his other board members to examine a new way of working.

There was acceptance across the board that a new role using his entrepreneurial flair would be more aligned to the business and his personal needs.

A new way of working was established where the senior executive could utilise his skills more effectively. His growing awareness of personal meaning and purpose had helped him self-correct and take each day as the same. He stopped feeling self-pity and decided that he needed to detail what his purpose in business was going to be in this chapter of his career. Once he made this step, lots of momentum occurred.

He soon realised how he could really find new ways of working and how he could give unconditionally to others. Over time he began to find new technological interests that he wanted to explore further. This led to new career opportunities and a refreshed approach to business. As things started to develop he took the decision to change careers into this new technology space.

The Defining Moment

He became much freer and happier with the decision to try something new that gave him more purpose and satisfaction. He started to reflect on his journey and felt that he had made real changes in the following areas. Firstly he felt more in control and had a real purpose to his work. He now had the room to take decisions on the business that were ordinarily ignored due in part to the size of the organisation but also who he was working for. Secondly, he loved the new technology space and had a genuine desire to connect new technologies to business opportunities. His visionary ideas had been lost and were being stunted and he didn't realise that part of his success was inspiring others to achieve more. He had got waylaid by the details of business operations. In his new role he was able to generate new learning and constantly innovate. Thirdly, he had begun to develop a diverse range of suppliers, customers and staff, which made each day very different. He had lost such variety and he had forgotten what it was like to strive doing something you enjoy. Finally, he simply had his mojo back. Now people needed and respected him. His business started to grow significantly and he could see a brighter future.

This individual, and many others, realised that just

surviving in their role was not enough. There was more to do. Our conversations allowed this man to reduce his self-centredness and fear. Instead, he began to think how he could better serve others. The by-product was that he was able to link people to new technologies. He became a business advisor to several companies needing accelerated growth. He became much more aligned and happier serving others. Their joy was like a magnet to others as they continued to inspire others to achieve more. They understood that serving others felt great. As a result, they paid great attention to working more selflessly. This created a self-fulfilling prophecy as their staff also grew as human beings. High performance was the natural by-product of this leadership style. He had discovered his purpose.

In conclusion, these examples clearly illustrate that having a purpose to serve others drives happiness in the workplace. Staff feel inspired, supported and, importantly, cared for. Such leadership care builds and sustains the health of any organisation.

Finding Your Purpose Following Career Transition

It is always difficult to see world-class athletes find a new direction when they have achieved their dreams or come to retirement in their sport. What happens next is the big question facing retiring athletes. What happens when all your dreams either come true or end? How do you cope when your direction stops? It is vital to recognise any transition in life, and it's an area I'm called to do a lot of work in. You can learn much from the world of sport in this respect. I know from my own experiences of retirement from professional cricket at the tender age of twenty-six that life throws up major obstacles.

For example, I thought what am I going to do now? What am I going to spend the rest of my life doing and how am I going to replace my passion with something else?

Having had the experience of retiring and having worked with many retiring sportsmen and women I have seen everything retirement has to offer. I've witnessed those that have been able to use their position of power and influence in their sport to transition to a new career, establish a new way of working and more importantly new dreams. The ultimate tonic for transition is having new dreams about what your purpose is in life post your first career. So the elite athlete who makes the smooth transition to a new career has had significant alternative dreams to what they have achieved so far, whereas the elite athletes who have no dreams beyond their passion for their sport suffer a huge amount upon retirement – whether it is voluntary or involuntary.

I have experienced many athletes and executives get into such isolation following retirement. Their dreams stop once their passion stops and they find it difficult to live. There are many examples of sportsmen and women who have spiralled out of control once they were either forced or chose to retire. You only have to look at cricket and see the demise of top England cricketers once the notion of retirement is aired. Boxers, footballers, snooker players (to name a few) all suffer from all sorts of potential addictions following retirement. You only have to read the newspapers to read who the latest sports star is to fall by the wayside following the demise of their career, be it addiction to drink, drugs, relationship failures etc.

Or they may sadly fall into mental illness through prolonged stress and anxiety that causes depression or at times suicide.

In order to prevent this happening to individuals, there needs to be an educational programme to help them get immersed into establishing new dreams and new directions in their lives based on how they can serve others. This needs to happen at the start of their careers and it's something I feel passionate about. They have to accept the notion that it is simply unhealthy to be defined by your sport or job. Your self-regard needs to be built on so much more. Such individuals have to accept this is dangerous and must change. This important self-correction will represent a significant shift in your level of self-protection and self-care. Here the individual begins to find ways to feel good about themselves not based simply on what they do but what they give for the benefit of others. They learn to build self-regard in other things they love doing. They find ways to spend time doing things that make them feel happy. This is like taking a vitamin each day to re-wire new dreams into their life that build energy and enthusiasm. The invitation is to go deeper with favourite hobbies or activities. For example, for one student it was going for a walk along his local beach without his phone. For one athlete it was doing hot yoga in perfect locations around the world. For one executive it was going for long road cycle rides and completing the London to Paris road bike race. For one parent it was collecting fine pieces of art. From all these hobbies and activities these individuals found a way of counterbalancing whatever their biggest passions were in life. Some even progressed such hobbies and activities into opportunities for work. For example, the senior executive invested in a bike manufacturer. This meant he initiated other interests outside of his main work, which helped build his feelings of self worth and self-acceptance. He had other things he could do if his current world was turned upside down.

In conclusion, as a society, the negative effect of retirement needs to be addressed. Retirement eats away at our self-esteem, particularly enforced or early retirement. Our responsibility is to ensure our levels of self-care are high so that we always have something we can give to others and replace what we retire from. This 'something else' should be focused on what you can do to help others. Here there is a shift from self-importance to a selfless state. The key question is: 'what can I do to contribute to others in society?' How can I be helpful to others? Individuals who are about to retire need to use their skills to give back to others and find a personal meaning in their life once more. This is especially true of athletes who should be clear on how they can serve others whilst performing. Something very special always comes out of this type of thinking. It's not just about trying to be positive; it's a much deeper search about what you can give back to society. What do you take from your talent and experiences in sport to contribute in a far deeper way than you could have imagined?

Retirement must not be seen as the end of something, but the start of a new passion or dream in life. Such dreams are the lifeblood of sustaining happiness in life. This happiness is contagious and inspires others whilst also helping the retired person renew their sense of purpose. An exit plan allows the sportsman or woman to take the difficult journey of how to shift from self-importance to a position of selflessness in order to find his or her future purpose. This process allows for the unravelling of specific psychological battles that eat away at self-esteem and inhibit happiness, freedom and success in life. By asking the right questions, some athletes are challenged to dig deeper to find a greater purpose beyond their sport, whilst others simply reject change out of hand and become fixated on sticking with what they know.

Whatever the athlete chooses, they must have the same dreams, passion and commitment they had during their playing days. They must find new ways to think in order to resolve that 'something missing' element that retirement brings.

My ABC Plan Example: A Second Snooker World Champion

The World Snooker Association asked me to run a series of personal development courses for the best young snooker players in the world. The Young Players of Distinction (YPD) was created. It brought the best young snooker players together to discuss how they could make the most of their careers. Out of this process a number of them have consistently been in the world's top ten, winning many titles. It was great to influence the development of these young players.

1. Awareness

One player, in particular, had amazing support from his dad in his snooker development. His dad's vision for what his son could contribute to the global game of snooker was clear for all to see. This player had a purpose in life. From the age of eight, his parents bought him a little snooker table for Christmas and his dream began. They also allowed him to play snooker full-time from the age of thirteen, having a tutor to help with his home study. By sixteen he had turned professional. There was total dedication and commitment to becoming the best snooker player in the world, practising seven hours a day and playing tournaments at the weekend. He made a complete choice to become a world-class snooker player. From a young age he had been preparing for snooker greatness.

This was evident throughout the YPD programme, with everything done as if he were already one of the best in the world. Snooker training sessions were designed as if the players were at the Crucible – the home of snooker. During these sessions he would showcase his immense talent for the game. It was very obvious that snooker was in his blood – it was his life, and he had absolute clarity about his role in snooker both on and off the table. His driven purpose in life was to become a world snooker champion. In addition, he also wanted to be remembered as one of the finest players the game has ever known. His dad worked tirelessly in a bid for this to happen. His dad was a senior executive in snooker and trained and drilled his son over many years in order to make progress towards his dream.

His clarity of purpose about what the game required was second to none and he knew how to put the final touches together to help his son achieve his dreams. The YPD programme was his brainchild, as a way of helping young quality players understand how to conduct themselves both on and off the table. During the YPD sessions, over several days at Lilleshall National Sports Centre, this player's game was exceptional. He was also a leader in discussions about his vision for the game. As a result, he would hold court on issues affecting play as well as issues affecting the brand reputation of snooker. His thinking was much more about being a custodian of the game and how to look after it for generations to come. The group discussions were lively as you may well expect as a group of top performers were locking horns on their views of the game. It was great to see. He was always incisive and clear. It was obvious that he had been groomed for stardom. His father was constantly enabling him to see the quality standard required to play any sport. For example, while aged only ten he was challenged by his dad to bounce golf balls up and down on his club to see if he could outscore him – he couldn't. From an early age his dad was instrumental in helping him cultivate a dream, love and mastery for developing high-level skills.

His vision and dream of becoming a world champion from an early age meant his knowledge and understanding of the game from all perspectives was high. In those early formative years he was clearly a leader in the sport. This was evident throughout the YPD programme that one session on personal branding led him to be nicknamed the 'Ambassador'. So to be watching him several years later living out his dream of being in the final of the World Snooker Championships was tremendous. To see him at close quarters win two qualifying matches together with beating three former world champions, including one who was invited along to the YPD course to share his knowledge and experience of long and distinguished career, was amazing. However, after the first day he was trailing his opponent and was appearing frustrated – something he had not shown throughout the tournament. He was clearly very stressed given how far he had come in the tournament only to be in a losing position overnight. It was obvious to him that he needed to play with the same freedom and purpose he had shown throughout the early stages of the championship.

2. Belief

Now he was on the brink of becoming world champion as a qualifier, which was an unbelievable achievement in itself. This could only happen if he accepted he needed to get back on purpose. He needed to accept things had changed in the final and he was trying to hard to win it. That evening he became more open about how he had played in the final and the factors impacting his play. This was an important period for going back to basics and truly believing in his brand of snooker. A no-fear purpose-driven mind-set was accepted as the way forward when play resumed the following day. He had approached the whole tournament with no fear and a childlike sense of enthusiasm. He had no expectation other than to do his best and play his best snooker and go for all his shots. He was eager to continue to take on the impossible long shots and play with fluidity.

3. Correction

After beating one of the world champions in the quarter finals, thoughts of winning had started to creep in. By the final he knew they were affecting his play. That evening he went through a process of self-correction. Here he got perspective and a desire to play with freedom, fun and purpose. The self-correction was in evidence the next day and he went for all his shots and completely took control of the second day's early exchanges.

The Defining Moment

Like every world champion I've ever worked with, I am always taken aback by the fact that elite athletes are always surprised when they become the best in the world.

It represents the World Champion Contradiction. On the one hand, the snooker player dreamt of becoming world champion, while on the other hand, there was disbelief when he actually achieved it. The shock and lack of belief that it has really happened always surprises me. For this player it didn't feel real for a good while after. It still felt like a dream. It was his first major final and he was world champion – wow! Even though he had sacrificed all his life to make this happen he still felt he had come from nowhere to be a world champion. Every world champion I've known or worked with experiences this paradox.

Your ABC Plan: Living Your Dreams in Life

'Living your dreams' requires hard work to establish what they are. You will need to pay attention to your dreams. So many of us are not used to spending time thinking about what really makes us happy. At times, we just take what we are offered. I have hundreds of examples of people who are stuck doing something they don't enjoy but it fills a hole, either financially or emotionally. Are you doing something that is not absolutely fulfilling you? Are you frustrated with life? If so, this is an indication that your ego is holding you to ransom. On the one hand, you don't enjoy what you are doing, while on the other, you tell yourself that you can do nothing about it. You stop living your life with that childlike enthusiasm. Can you find something in life that gives you that childlike eagerness? Are you doing it in your life today? If not, you need to reignite your passion and accept that what you tell yourself is a form of fear. As a result, can you answer the following questions: what inspires you in life? Do you know what your passion is in life? Do you find it easy or hard to find meaning in your life?

What are your immediate thoughts regarding these questions?

I am always fascinated and surprised when asking world champions these questions. They are interesting people to work with as they have achieved their life-long dreams. It begs the question of what next? What do you do after you achieve your dreams? Generally you witness a range of feelings from contentment to ambiguity. How could someone at the top of their game feel anxious about what they are doing? This is an interesting place to be and an interesting one to investigate as it gives us a window into what really satisfies us emotionally. I have found that world-class performers who focus on winning from a self-interest perspective show signs of emotional fragility even though they are perceived as winners in life. I'm always surprised to work with some of the best in the world who appear frustrated that their achievements are not enough.

A crazy paradox; on the one hand, society perceives them as the ultimate icons of success, while, on the other hand, they feel alone and unfulfilled. They have all the trappings of success but emotionally they crave more. They feel they are only as good as their next win. They have their eyes locked on their next win as if they are addicts looking for their next fix. I have witnessed how this can manifest in dark and dysfunctional behaviour such as alcoholism, drug taking, gambling or illicit affairs etc. They have everything but emotionally feel lonely and empty. They strive to fill their emotional void with whatever stops them thinking. They try to numb their pain. Consequently, there is something limiting about winning. It is simply not enough. We need more as human beings. Can you identify a time when your success generated an anti-climactic feeling? Do you agree or disagree with the idea that winning is not enough? How do you fill your emotional void in life?

What is the answer? As I've been saying throughout this book, which I hope you will embrace and never forget, the answer lies in working out how you can win for others. This gives your life true purpose and meaning. It stimulates a childlike aliveness that is infectious. You need to start today and think about how you can live your life from the perspective of serving others by the way you win at something. Does anything immediately come to mind?

This is an enlightening realisation that freedom, happiness and sustained success manifest from a desire to win for the benefit of others. Here we need to take up the challenge of putting our oxygen mask on in order to breathe life into becoming more selfless. This becomes a self-fulfilling prophecy: as you pay attention to win for a reason bigger than you it automatically improves your own life. It is as if the airplane steward is reading the emergency procedures to you. You must put your mask on before you can help yourself or your children. The same is true here. You need a high level of self-care to ensure that you find a way of winning that serves others. I'm always intrigued by one particular international cricketer, who, on the final day of a five-day match, when the conclusion to the game is in sight, always appears freer to perform, striking the ball with perfect rhythm and grace. Why does this freedom occur now? Well, quite simply, he feels much better about performing his role to create the win for his team and nation. He chooses a selfless batting mode that enables him to play with greater freedom than when he is playing to achieve a score for himself. Can you think of a time when you performed better at something when you knew it was helping others more than you?

My view is clear: we only have an allocated amount of time on this earth, as, unfortunately, death always presents us with the fundamentals of life. We must ensure we pursue life for the right reasons. We must be determined to find our true purpose in life. It is not money, fame or success that defines us. Instead it is what we leave behind when we depart this world. Therefore, it is imperative that you live your dreams to the fullest. I have discovered that you gain the most from life by serving a purpose greater than you. What is your purpose beyond you? How can you serve others? This demands you think about your dreams in relation to helping others to become inspired by you. You owe it to yourself to get the very most from the purpose of your life. It should not be lived in vain. You need to live out your dreams and not succumb to fear and emotional pain. Instead, you must unravel your emotional pain and blockages. This will leave you more aligned and less vague and indecisive. You need a clear destination for why you do what you do in the pursuit of winning that benefits others. It is only low self-esteem that stops us pursuing our dreams for the benefit of others.

What can you do to appreciate your precious commodity of time and serve others with your winning? What can you leave behind? What difference did you make to others' lives? How do you want to be remembered? What stops you chasing your dreams? What are your fears about dreaming? How are you going to serve others in life? Do you accept that serving others with your winning is the key to your purpose and happiness? Are you living your values and beliefs that winning for the benefit of others is your true purpose in life? Can you change your way of thinking to support others? What contribution have you made to inspiring others? These are big, big questions and will take time to digest and regulate. What are your immediate thoughts?

ABC Plan – 'Living Your Dream in Life

Understanding your reflective practice

So, by working through your own Awareness, Belief and Correction (ABC) Plan you will be in a better position to understand your true purpose in life.

Awareness (A): Purposeful Attitude

– You will need to examine your attitude towards what your purpose in life is. Do you agree or disagree that you know what your purpose in life is when you hunt winning at something? How aware are you of your purpose in life? If you are unaware of your direction, you will most definitely be operating egotistically or selfishly.

Belief (B): Purposeful Behaviour

You will need to assess your purpose-driven behaviour. Do you ignore what your purpose is with significant people while you are doing something important? Are you able to accept your purpose driven behaviour in life? If you ignore your direction, you are almost certainly functioning with self-importance or selfishly.

Correction (C): Purposeful Values and Beliefs

You will need to consider what your underlying values and beliefs about the direction of your life are. You will need to consider how you can align your attitudes, behaviours, values and beliefs in order to embrace your purpose in life. If you choose to cultivate an ABC Personal Change Plan you will actively seek to understand your purpose in your life. This is an essential self-correction needed to understand that serving others lends support to what your purpose is in life. Shifting from a winning for oneself (selfish) to winning for others (selfless) perspective will give you vital data in understanding and determining your direction in life. This will give you a deeper level of joy and contentment.

Are you willing and committed to stop, look and listen to your internal traffic regarding what your purpose is in life?

If yes, it requires reflection and thinking about what thoughts and feelings are invoked when you pursue winning in life.

'Living Your Dream in Life':

Helping people to face the question of what their purpose is in life, is always very interesting and rewarding. I have had many discussions with lots of people about what their purpose is. Sometimes this is easy as I experience these individuals contemplating their lot and their direction in life. You can always see the cogs turning as they search for their purpose beyond their work. I invite people to explore how they could better impact the world they live in. Some look with bewilderment and surprise as they try to process what their purpose is beyond themselves. For example, when asked about how their talents are being used for the benefit of others they appear puzzled, with a blank expression, as they realise they don't really know and that their superficial answers fall on deaf ears.

As a result, they are challenged to genuinely explore how their talent and skills can best serve others even more in life. I ask them the following key question:

How does the way you currently serve others demonstrate your true purpose in life?

This always stimulates much discussion and debate about life and how their skills could be better utilised for the benefit of others. I have discovered that it is almost impossible to understand your true purpose without understanding how you are contributing to enhancing other people's lives.

Helping people understand their gifts and how to clarify their purpose is always tough but inspiring. Below are some examples:

- Helping a global senior executive realise that others found him inspirational in his ability to provide transformational leadership. This clarified his purpose in life. As a result, he re-discovered his passion to encourage others in business. He is currently supporting new technology and fast-growing companies to accelerate their growth.

- Supporting a Managing director as he transitioned into a new career beyond corporate life. Through our discussions he developed a greater understanding about what others gained from his leadership. This allowed him to consider how he could meet the needs of others within his new career. Today, he is supporting business leaders within the sports industry to inspire more young people to engage in sport.

- Helping a professional snooker player realise how his strength in dealing with several life-threatening illnesses gave hope and inspiration to people across the world, enabling him to see the bigger picture beyond winning for one's self. He began to appreciate that he had a vital contribution to make to society through his battle with his illnesses. Today, he is not only performing at his best and winning tournaments but he is writing a book to share his story and encourage all cancer patients.

All these individuals, and many others, have come to the realisation that being self-absorbed not only leads to unhappiness but also to poor results. When they were able to find how they could truly be of benefit to others, they instantly became freer, happier and more successful in life. Their joy is now like a magnet to others as they continued to inspire others to find their own purpose. They understood that serving others felt great. As a result, they paid great attention to working more selflessly. This created a self-fulfilling prophecy as others flourished. In conclusion, these examples clearly illustrate that you can only truly find your purpose once you establish how others gain from your gifts.

ABC Plan Summary

Firstly, I would like to summarise where we are up to regarding the activities you have performed. In Step One, you have pressed your own TV remote control in order to see how much you listen when you pursue winning in life; what did the data reveal? In Step Two, you began the process of smiling at your errors; what did you errors tell you? In Step Three, you took time to find a Special Place to explore what you avoid in life; what did taking the time to do this reveal? In Step Four, you examined the difference between what you feel and what you do; what did you discover about the degree of separation you experience in life? In Step Five, you explored how much fun you are having in life; what did you discover about yourself regarding how much fun you have? In Step Six, you explored how much you give to others in life; what did you discover about yourself regarding how much you give to others. In this **seventh step**, you will explore what your purpose in life is, starting with following questions:

- *Are you aware of what your purpose in life is?*
- *How do you go about finding what your purpose is in life?*
- *Are your dreams in life aligned to what you give to others?*

- Are you living your dreams when you are pursuing winning?
- What is the link between purpose and unconditional giving?
- Do you see the benefit of having a purpose in life?
- Do you get excited about your purpose in life?

Step Seven: Living Your Dream in Life

Through the above examples and the questions, what have you discovered about purpose? What did you enjoy about gaining greater clarity regarding your purpose?

Write a list of things you do to help your community – defined as any group of people that benefit from your unselfish act of serving them. It might be your local church or your local football club. It may be helping a national charity or supporting your village fete. Put the list in order, starting with who you serve the most with your generosity down to who you serve the least with your generosity.

- What pattern emerges from how you serve your community?
- Who would you like to serve more?
- What else can you do for your community?
- What are the differences between the ways you serve different communities?
- Do you think the way you serve your community gives a good indication of what your purpose in life is?
- What can you do to serve your community even more?

Regardless of whether you are playing sport or in business or education or at home with your family, chasing winning increases the likelihood that you will take rather than give. Such selfishness increases our level of taking from others in life; we feel others owe us. Here our desire is to get what we need from others. This is our ego taking over and it occurs especially when the pressure is on. What do you give when the pressure is on? What do you tell yourself? This is your ego operating. In living your dream activity you must learn to serve your community first. Do you have a purpose through serving your community? In living your dream activity, consider your thoughts regarding the following questions:

- What was your initial response or reaction to serving your community with who you are?
- Do you ignore or hide how you serve your community?
- How do you go about reconciling differences between serving your community and pursuing individual success in life?
- Do you resist serving your community?
- Does it feel uncomfortable to focus on how you serve your community?
- What does serving your community tell you about yourself?
- How do you tolerate others taking from how you serve your community?
- How do you behave when you are serving your community in life?

- What did you discover about your level of selfishness by the way you serve your community?

Purpose Mindfulness

Imagine a world where you felt absolutely free and happy to serve your community! Here you are simply rewarded for being kind to not only yourself but more importantly others. Your life is about enabling others to live more happily in their community. Everyone praises you for how you help others in the community. You feel respected and you give respect. You are tolerant and truthful to others. You are totally open. Others are open with you and are totally satisfied with what you give them and the community. You have a deep sense of your personal meaning in everything you do, especially your community work. You are who you want to be and appreciated by others for how you serve. Through Step Seven, you will be having it all. You will be living your dream. You will gain both individual expertise in what you do as well as extending collective excellence throughout the community you serve. How would you answer the following questions:

1. *What do you do differently as a result of thinking more unselfishly about how you can serve your community?*
2. *What can you do to shift your thinking from an individual to community perspective?*
3. *How do you go about aligning your differences between striving to win for oneself and striving to win for a community?*

4. *How does it feel to serve others more in your life?*
5. *How does it feel to receive respect for helping others?*
6. *How much fun do you think you can have in this world?*
7. *What do you have to do differently in reality to live more for a community?*

So, which way does your coin end up? Do you focus on 'no purpose' or 'purpose', especially when you are doing something important? I have discovered that serving your community first is vital to increased health, happiness and purpose. I have many experiences of seeing others serve more and improve many elements of their life. In so doing it creates momentum for others to do the same. Their service to others reduces fear, as they feel more free and happy as a person. This transformation inspires others to do the same and get the most from their life. Serving others is what the best in the world do intuitively. Having no clarity about how you serve others puts us into a selfish mode and leads to long-term negative health consequences.

Please select which statement best reflects you when you are about to do something important in life: *'I'm not sure what direction I'm going in,'* or, *'I'm absolutely clear on the purpose behind what I do.'*

Choice 1. 'I'm not sure what direction I'm going in'
No purpose mind-set: Not understanding your purpose is driven by ego (self-importance). You lack clarity about how you can serve your community. You are individually

focused, paying attention to what you need to do to win for yourself. Here your aim is to win in order to get the love and approval of others. You are selfish and see life as a battle for survival. You enjoy the feedback and recognition from others for your individual success. You don't focus on what your purpose is. Instead, you are self-centred on what you can achieve for yourself. You feel people should support you as you strive for success in life. You have a win-at-all-costs mind-set. You work hard to cross the line on a day-to-day basis. Your performance is inconsistent as winning for yourself is your focus. Your confidence is affected when you don't win. You get upset at being judged by others.

Choice 2. 'I'm absolutely clear on the purpose behind what I do'

Purpose mind-set: Focusing on serving your community is without ego driven. You are eager to serve your community in order that it flourishes. You are open, stable and interact effectively with those in and outside your community. This makes you feel free and happy with all that you do. You have clarity regarding your vision over how you can help your community. You appreciate there is a bigger purpose for supporting your team or community. You are ambitious about serving your community and supporting its impact on people. You are kind to yourself and others. You get immense pleasure out of helping the community. You see serving it as a priority and an important part of your life. The community appreciates and is inspired by your support. It encourages others to follow.

The community gains a lot from your presence and it is keen to extend kindness as much as possible. You are not selfish and you strive to encourage others to be more selfless with what they do. You are excited by the challenge of serving a community. Helping your community is very natural way of showing warmth and care to others. You have a high degree of self-care, which is a fundamental part of understanding your purpose in life. You gain immense joy out of finding your purpose in life through how you serve your community.

Conclusion

In conclusion, how do you react or respond to the invitation to serve your community? Do you feel free to serve your community? If not, what stops you serving your community? Your reaction or response to helping your community highlights your level of selflessness versus selfishness. Do you agree? When you self-correct your level of serving your community, how does it make you feel?

What are your examples of self-correcting your kindness and service to your community?

24

Building Your Personal Legacy

• • •

Life is a performance demanding that we win. From a mother watching her new-born sleeping, to a teacher assessing a pupil's results both in the classroom and on the sports field, to a boss monitoring his staff's sales targets – throughout our lives, from childhood to adulthood, we are constantly under the gaze of others interested in how we perform. We learn from an early age that we are all under sharp focus from others and that winning, regardless of what we do, will give us their much-needed love and support.

The aim of this book was to challenge your approach to winning, and you were invited to explore 'what you tell yourself', especially under pressure, when you were doing something important. Did you find you were able to commit to the process? Or did you find it too uncomfortable to look so deeply at yourself? Regardless of your response, you will have discovered that you need complete willingness to look in the mirror and ask yourself difficult questions.

Over the years of working with many individuals across many different environments, I've been overwhelmed by people who are genuinely prepared to understand one, some or all of the seven characteristics of ego as well as the Leadership withoutEGO® Model. My hope is that you can also show the same level of commitment to understanding these character-istics in a similar way. With this new level of understanding of your ego, you'll be willing to cultivate your awareness by digging deeper into unravelling the impact of each charac-teristic in your life, whether it is in sport, business, education or your day-to-day activities. You will now be able to grow awareness and accept what you choose to tell yourself while doing something important. As a result of such inner open-ness, you'll be able to choose the necessary self-correction in improving your approach under significant stress.

With everyone who has been through the **Detox Your Ego** programme, it is clear that his or her attitude, behaviour, values and beliefs have become aligned. It is always very rewarding to see how eager people become to learn new things and experiences. Committed individuals show child-like enthusiasm. My own inability to understand the impact of these seven characteristics of ego was one of the reasons for my underachievement in cricket. Interestingly, I found that these factors were also present in others in varying degrees. In fact, regardless of whether you have focus on one's self or others in your pursuit of winning, the process of becoming more aware of these seven characteristics of ego in life leads us to greater freedom, happiness and success.

So, how did it feel answering the in-depth questions asked in this book? You have been asked to focus on in-depth ques-tions through the forty Stop, Look and Listen elements; the Leadership withoutEGO® Model and during the ABC Plans, as well as, throughout the general text. The central aim was to examine 'what you tell yourself'; these questions helped you find a more value-based way of living, by gaining a greater appreciation of the personal meaning underlying what you do. You have a duty to ask yourself difficult questions regarding what you do; self-reflection over these questions and talking through your thoughts, feelings and actions with others is key to deepening your self-awareness. I have witnessed many people shift from just saying what others want to hear, to saying what they really think and feel; students, parents, teachers, executive and athletes learn to talk more openly in group discussion. I have found that people feel really positive when they are able to confront their own 'elephant in the room' or their very own uncomfortable truth. In all these circumstances, individuals are always keen to understand their emotions at a much deeper level, especially in sport.

I'm sure we can all remember many examples of great sportsmen and women who get near to the finishing line and appear to throw it away. Who can forget seeing various cricketers getting bowled in the last over to lose the final? Or the great golfers who throw away a lead going down the final stretch in a major championship? What about the athlete leading in an Olympic race, only to fall at the last hurdle or lap? Or the footballer who misses a vital penalty at a major event, like a World Cup? Or a snooker player who misses the last ball to lose a final? Or what about the boxer on his way to victory, only to be caught by a knockout punch in the last round of the World Championship fight? In each case, from what seemed to be an unassailable lead, the performer appears to throw it away by not being able to cope under intense pressure – commonly known as choking. We get captivated and engrossed with their roller coaster of emotion and uncertainty about what will happen next. We ponder whether a performer will choke or not. This makes compelling and fascinating viewing, but at what cost to the individual involved? I have seen unprecedented levels of stress and burnout amongst sporting stars who didn't ask themselves the right questions to establish a greater understanding of the emotional distress they experienced. In every sport I've consulted in I have had to deal with individuals suffering some form of despair resulting from their blind pursuit of winning for one's self.

Consequently, I encourage you to openly share your ideas and impact of the Leadership withoutEGO® Model with others. Whether you have one person to share with, or a group of five or six, sharing your thoughts and self-observations can help you consider operating more selflessly within your community. Sharing our thoughts in a supportive group – almost akin to an extended family – is an important part of continuing your detox, as this process will reveal important data regarding some of your deepest fears, hopes and aspirations. In team settings, I have seen both professional sportsmen and women benefit from sharing thoughts about what they've been avoiding with others. I've had many encounters helping executives understand their emotions at work in order to tackle their work pressure from a new perspective; it's always great to see the weight lifted as they begin to unburden themselves of their difficulties. They accept that there may not be immediate solutions but the ability to talk their problems through in a safe environment is a significant step in the right direction. In all these cases, from both an individual and team perspective, sharing their problems gave them insight into finding a real solution.

I have discovered at the heart of these personal observations, reflections and discussions that our deepest fears manifest in our actions. We are either wittingly or unwittingly driven by the fear of *not being good enough* or the fear of being *rejected by others*. These represent our two deepest fears. In a recent BBC show, a former England captain highlighted the effects of not winning as captain; Australia retained the Ashes and the captain, by his own admission, went into depression. Over the years, I have played with and against many cricketers who experience similar issues and fall into depression as a result of life in the sport. Unfortunately, cricket has one of the highest rates of depression and suicide of any sport as players find it difficult to reconcile their needs to win with transition and retirement from the game. Retirement brings a level of isolation. I have also found this occurring across different sports with a number of other sportsmen and women who, at some stage in their careers, suffer some level of distress regarding retirement. It helps us to get close to and embrace our deepest fears; we need to learn to find a way to celebrate them if we are going to conquer them. This will enable us to live life to the fullest and experience high levels of joy as a result of looking more inwardly.

I have witnessed those that look outwardly to find happiness; such individuals believe that joy can be found through wealth, fame and celebrity. However, as we have seen with star sports people, successful tech billionaires and movie stars, there is a realisation that their happiness cannot be gained through winning and success alone. There is an anomaly here that, while these individuals appear to have everything, they in fact experience feelings of isolation, loneliness and being trapped by their achievements. One only has to flick through the tabloids to see the stories associated with celebrities and sporting stars – everything is watched, scrutinised and judged. Celebrities and sporting stars begin to feel anxious and mistrustful of those around them, they get overly concerned with the lack of privacy and try all sorts of things to maintain control. Such a media spotlight can have very harmful effects. I have seen a steady growth of addictive behaviour from alcohol to gambling to partying in order to relieve some of the stress.

It is always fantastic to see people take up the challenge of looking in the mirror and finding joy in what they see. While this is difficult, the challenge is for us all to learn to accept what we discover about ourselves. In so doing, we are in a strong position to make the necessary self-corrections, to move towards aligning our inner, outer and transformational ego. Our ability to have fun is driven by the alignment of what we feel with what we do. If we have misalignment we need to develop a greater sense of acceptance in order to close the gap between our feelings and actions. Perhaps this process is part of the much talked-about 'third wave' of cognitive behavioural therapy (CBT), where individuals are invited to embrace their difficulties in life instead of trying to eliminate or reduce them. For example, the student finds a way to welcome the stress of his or her exam pressure; or the athlete explores how he or she can generate new ideas on how to run the final lap in order to perform at their best. Finally, the executive establishes new ways of addressing conflict with staff by finding ways to enhance their relationships.

It is fantastic to see an organisation's CEO take up the challenge of building a critical mass of leaders who have more fun with their work. They develop a greater appreciation of the collective excellence of their organisation – the performance and results begin to shine as each member starts to enjoy working together. Here the profit-at-all-costs greedy attitude is replaced and the organisation really starts to have more fun by embracing how it can serve its community better and in so doing make more profit.

It begs the question that if we could bottle this fun mindset culture, perhaps we could reduce the millions and millions of working days lost in Britain due to work-related stress, depression or anxiety. Both the individual and organisational benefit of a more fun environment would be enormous. In contrast, I regularly see people at work who are miserable; clearly, they are present but not really performing. This represents yet another indication of the mismatch between what we want to happen and what actually is happening. This may well get worse as the new economic climate means individuals struggle with performance and health problems, amidst fears for the security of their jobs. As a result, organisational leaders and staff need to develop greater emotional awareness to shift this pattern. They need to improve their psychological flexibility or acceptance in understanding workplace stress. In such cases, the Leadership withoutEGO® approach reduces anxiety and gives each individual greater freedom to have fun in their stressful situation in the workplace.

Without doubt the ability to unconditionally give to others is both difficult and rewarding at the same time. Unconditional giving makes us feel vulnerable, just as if we were at altitude. We have a moral and ethical duty to pay attention to what we do for others, even though it is difficult, as we flicker between self-interest and caring for others. The modern world pays emphasis on our individuality but it is about us paying close attention to what we are doing for the collective good. Here we will be measured by our actions – that is, do our actions indicate a selfless contribution to our community? Or do our actions show how individual and selfish we are? When we are able to see others enjoying how we serve, we begin to truly get a deeper level of appreciation regarding our purpose in life.

For example, our next generation need greater levels of support and care so that they can live their dreams and contribute better to society at large. Young people are finding it difficult to get the support from others, especially those from disaffected backgrounds. With the global economic downturn, young people are feeling isolated as the future looks uncertain. As a result, we are seeing a significant increase in mental health issues within our young who are feeling a lack of direction and purpose. They are more exposed to stress and anxiety like never before. In cities around the world we are seeing a significant increase in disillusionment felt by young people cut off from the mainstream. Young people, like athletes and executives, need a renewed way of thinking so that they can gain alignment and recalibrate what success in life truly is. Here they need to cultivate an appreciation of what they can do to generate learning so that they may give more to society. Admittedly, they need to see and experience more unconditional giving from their stakeholders; whether that be schools, colleges, universities, businesses, political institutions, local authorities, prisons, churches, charities and sporting organisations. I could go on – we all have a responsibility to become more ambassadorial and transformational within our community.

We need to talk and create a vehicle for leaders to develop their transformational ego so that we can contribute greater joy to our society. It is vital that we all play a role in improving our wellbeing, as the World Health Organisation states that suicide is the second highest cause of death in 15-29-year-olds. We need to establish a new selfless way of thinking where we can focus on winning for others first – our community. Whether we define our community as our family or local area or team or group at work, we must act to serve them first.

The ultimate question for us all is, have you reached the summit in life? That is, can you effectively see what your purpose in life is? It's extremely difficult to answer and involves proactively seeking feedback from others to shed light on what you are best suited to doing. Consequently, you will need to establish how others can benefit from what you give unconditionally. What they say will reveal your purpose in life. When we have a critical mass of people with a mind-set of serving others we begin to see complete transformations within our communities.

Serving others is the right thing to do, and you will need to be committed to finding a way to establish this if you are going to feel free, happy and successful in what you do. For example, one senior executive really enjoyed designing ways of working that allowed others to flourish; based on his own experience of stress at the highest level of organisations. The feedback about his style of leadership was so positive that he decided to make a career change so that he could spend more time influencing and persuading others about dealing with transitions in their lives. As a result, he set up a coaching and mentoring programme for adolescent children, giving them both space and time to embrace a number of difficult transitions. These students enjoyed talking through shared experiences concerning change in their lives.

What would it feel like to live in a society where we were

all truly valued for the people we are, not the people we're expected to be? Where we could give unconditionally to anyone without fear of rejection or humiliation? In this world we would be happy and free to express ourselves to the fullest; there would be no criticism, rejection or judgement. A world of deep spiritual purpose, of understanding of our gifts, and our value to others. Here our best would be good enough now. No psychological battles or wars, just love, peace and contentment. There would be no stress-induced anxiety or depression. There would also be no interpersonal conflict and everyone would be resilient and able to resolve issues effectively. Those that should lead would deliver their gifts, while those that should follow would execute their talents as well.

What a wonderful, special place. Could we create this world? Could you contribute to make it possible? Now that you've progressed through the Seven Steps, experienced your own version of the World Champion Contradiction, and detoxed your ego, this is the time to look to the future.

I invite you to take responsibility and be accountable to yourself and your community with your newfound level of appreciation of yourself and your gifts. Continue your journey being mindful at all times of the seven characteristics of your ego. Revisit these Seven Steps in this book on a regular basis and always be inquisitive regarding your ego: ask questions of it and contemplate the answers as part of your daily routine. I thoroughly recommend making time to find a small group, where you can share your views and reflections on the Seven Steps and gain a greater appreciation and understanding of yourself and others.

Most of all, enjoy your journey to freedom from what bound and stifled you before – the relentless need to win. Set all previous misconceptions of what your ego meant aside and embrace the mantra 'my best is good enough now'.

If there's one point I would leave you to reflect on, it would be that it's only when you serve others with your gifts that you will truly find your purpose and live a more fulfilled life.

I wish you the best life possible and abundant freedom, happiness and success in all you do.

If you would like to to understand more, and for some additional online resources that might assist you, then please visit the Leadership withoutEGO® website: *www.withoutego.com*

About the Author

. . .

Steven Sylvester is a former professional cricketer who is now a leading Chartered Psychologist providing a new approach to human performance across a range of individuals and teams in professional sport, business, and life. He also played Academy football for Oxford United. After completing a first degree in psychology at London University's Goldsmiths College, he began his career in professional sport, playing first class cricket for Middlesex and Nottinghamshire. After choosing to retire from professional cricket, he completed further academic intensive training with a Master's degree in psychology to become a Chartered Psychologist with the British Psychological Society (BPS). He has now achieved the status of Associate Fellow within the BPS for his contribution to psychology. He is also a Registered Practitioner Psychologist with the Health & Care Professions Council (HCPC). Combined with his own experience as a performer, this informed his practice as he began to consult with numerous elite athletes, helping them develop into world-class performers. A number of defining moments occurred when several of these elite athletes became world champions. Today, elite athletes, senior executives, students, teachers, parents and others are now utilising Steven's unique Leadership withoutEGO® framework to accelerate and enhance their performance and life.